360°
A Revolution
Of Black Poets

Number: ________

Commemorative Edition

September 11 - 12, 1998

360°
A Revolution Of Black Poets

Edited by
Kalamu ya Salaam
with
Kwame Alexander

Black Words™

in association with

Runagate Press

New Orleans

Books are available in bulk at discount prices. Single copies are available prepaid direct from the publisher.

Published by
BlackWords
P. O. Box 21, Alexandria, VA 22313
(703) 912-1786 / blackwords@juno.com

in association with
Runagate Press
P. O. Box 52723, New Orleans, LA 70152-2723
(504) 523-4443 ext. 22 / runagate@aol.com

Design, layout and typesetting by: Runagate Press
Book composed in Stone Informal, Stone Sans, Stone Serif

Back Cover Photo (Kwame Alexander): Dawit Mulugeta
Back Cover Photo (Kalamu ya Salaam): Eric Waters

ISBN Commemorative Edition: 1-888018-14-3
ISBN Hard Cover Edition: 1-888018-12-7

Library of Congress Catalogue Card Number: 98-073644

Manufactured in the United States of America
10 9 8 7 6 5 4 3 2 1

Dedication

To and for Black poets everywhere
who understand and are committed to:
both art and struggle,
our people and the world,
an aesthetic that includes politics,
a politics which embraces art,
both the spoken and the written word,
and the inclusion of all the voices
which make up our 360° diversity
of human experiences, concerns and aspirations.

ashé

Acknowledgments

BlackWords™ and Runagate thank and send shouts out to:
All of the authors who graciously consented to the use of their poetry in this anthology. Some of the poems in this anthology have been previously published. The copyright for all poems are held by the individual authors of those poems. All poems are used by permission of the authors and their publishers.

BlackWords™ thanks and sends shouts out to:
the valued and valuable company partners, Irwin Alexis and Angela Boykin;
the supporting staff and volunteers, Stephanie Stanley, Carla Peterson and Ann Carlswell of the University of Maryland, Stacey Shelnut, Jiton Sharmayne Davidson, Marvin Hamilton, E. Ethelbert Miller, Sheila Alexis, Nandi Assata Alexander, Barbara Alexander, Mykel & Jahamare Stanley, Miles & Indigo Alexis, Christopher Downing, Rose and the entire Third World Press Family, Troy Johnson, William Jordan, Carolyn Joyner, Tebabu Assefa, The Gerimas and the Entire Mypeduh Family.

Runagate thanks and sends shouts out to:
our kkk-troika: Kysha N. Brown, Karen Celestan and Kalamu ya Salaam;
our hard working production team: Chandra Carriere, David Harrison,
Cassandra Lane, Marion Moore, Lynn Pitts, Carol Santos;
Kymberly Brown for the loan of a Mac monitor;
visual artists: Douglas Redd and Zouk (Kiini Ibura Salaam)
graphics design artist: Asante Salaam;
and to all who participated in the invention and implementation of "e-mail"!

Table of Contents

Table of Contents

Table of Contents

Table of Contents

Table of Contents

FORWARD: Evolution of a New Era in Black Words

1978. There is always something liberating about remembering and honoring the early times. The times of summers down South, Panther breakfasts, unlaced Adidas, and *Rapper's Delight.* The times that told us it was okay to dream, and even better if we woke up. The times that grounded us and signaled our direction. *Where we are headed may not be where we end up, but where we have been may tell us how to get there.*

Enter a new generation of Black poets, fed on breakbeats, nationalism and wide-eyed racism. Born amidst hard times (indeed, remember Koch?); but we grew, like Crown Heights tensions, we grew. Out of no excuses and neighbors who cared, came a generation of Black poets and writers, who, at least initially, gave a loving nod to our aesthetic predecessors by writing fire from our souls.

No matter how threatening our environments, we forged healing paths by reading Black. Langston taught us to laugh. Gwendolyn taught us to think. Claude Brown taught us to endure. Tom Feelings taught us to feel good about ourselves. No matter how often Ms. Morgan ignored our hand-waving frenzy or rejected our fourth-grade identities, we confidently claimed our heritage and pride in intricate rhymes and poems composed in basement ciphers and on street corners (way after the street lights went out). In these early times, we learned to be beautiful and bold, to remember history, to treasure and challenge tomorrows.

For this writer, these times began at 10 Claver Place in a three-story brick building that housed a health food store, a multi-purpose auditorium and a publishing and printing operation. This place where a young, prophetic word-warrior by the name of Haki R. Madhubuti (Don L. Lee) regularly captured in verse the struggle for identity, purpose and direction. This place where a fine, heart-instructed sisterpoet by the name of Sonia Sanchez often struck an intense blow to the familial in each and every revolutionary bone in the house. This place where a tall, outspoken Pan-African academic by the name of Dr. E. Curtis Alexander fused Ivy League-training with Paulo Freire to create a methodology for teaching functional Black art to Black children, while showing his son the inner workings of a newspaper and book publishing unit owned and operated by Black folks. This place called "The East" at 10 Claver Place, Brooklyn, New York.

The Easts of the past, from Watts to Washington, DC, gave us most of the necessary skills, tactics and ammunition to fight the ongoing war of that which really runs the world (as Haki Madhubuti often states): Ideas. In the mid-to-late eighties, our little minds exploded with Black creative energy on college campuses across the country. During this era, several social realities gave a significant jolt to the rallying voice of the emerging poets (many of whom were enrolled in college at the time): the Anti-Apartheid movement, the institutionalizing of Black Studies and the ever-present challenge of campus racism. This new generation of word-users echoed the surviving aesthetic that Addison Gayle wrote about twenty years ago:

> *We are today, in a Black cultural renaissance, in which perhaps, for the last time, Black nationalist writers will be able to project—to Black people— a sense of our unique, separate cultural identity, by resolving the dichotomy between art and function, thereby making art and function relevant to the Black Community.*

It is this liberating past that opened the doors for the word-warriors of my generation to breathe new air. Equipped with stilleto inkpens and bulletproof backpacks, we wield as weapons a literature balanced with personal challenge and community and cultural identity. Our verse, whether university-trained or performance-oriented is rooted in a continuum of undaunting commitment to our families and our people.

This current era of Black Words has unique sensibilities. Faced with the increased market-driven global economy, specifically as it relates to the dominance of entertainment over art, we poets often find ourselves pitting old expectations against new realities. *Everybody is conscious, but when we gonna eat?* Although these subjects are more often dealt with in the contemporary poetry, they did not come out of a vacuum. We are the direct literary descendants of the Black Arts Poets: Amiri Baraka, Mari Evans, Haki Madhubuti, Sonia Sanchez, Nikki Giovanni, Askia Toure, Sam Greenlee, June Jordan, Wanda Coleman, Larry Neal, Eugene Redmond, Carolyn Rodgers, Kalamu ya Salaam,

Foreword

The Last Poets, Jerry Ward, E. Ethelbert Miller, Keropatse Kgositile, Ntozake Shange, Quincy Troupe, and on and on.

We have among us emerging Black poets, a plethora of literary talent and potential: Thomas Sayers Ellis, wadud, Toni Asante Lightfoot, Kysha N. Brown, Tony Medina, Jessica Care Moore, Quraysh Ali Lansana, Glenis Redmond Sherer, Nadir Lasana Bomani, Shonda Buchanan, Tyehimba Jess, Kupenda Auset, DJ Renegade, asha bandele, Goldie Muhammad, Saul Williams, Ras Baraka, Kevin Powell, Michael Datcher, D-Knowledge, Stacey Lyn Evans, Ruth Forman, A.K. Toney, and on and on. If these writers (including this author) can avoid *ego-posturing* and the trappings of the ever-increasing trendy commercialization of the arts, we will undoubtedly be prepared to accept the inevitable task of moving Black poetry forward in the next millenium. All that remains is for us to do it.

***

1998. "360° A Revolution of Black Poets" is our modest effort to *do it.* "Our" represents the combined staff of the festival (BlackWords and Runagate), and the numerous other self-determined individuals and companies who joined our sincere efforts to bring a representative cross-generation of Black poets under one roof, on one stage, in the spirit of one love. 360° is first and foremost a festival of Black poetry and Black poets in America and abroad. In addition, 360° is a major anthology of forty dynamic Black poets (many of who are mentioned above); 360° is a video documentary on the past thirty years of Black poetry in this country. In keeping with the age-old tradition, which has received major media attention lately, 360° pays homage to the Spoken Word with a live compact disc. This is 360°: a multi-media institution spearheaded by a group of very together grass-roots organizers and entrepreneurs, very progressive academics, and more than forty "baaaad" poets who agreed to participate in this historic occasion with minimal remuneration .

The idea for 360° developed after I decided to start a publishing company that would provide publishing opportunities for the many talented literary voices of the Hip-Hop Generation. Thus BlackWords, Inc. was born. Through subsequent discussions (some more intense than others), with colleagues, friends and fellow poets, several key issues were put on the table relative to the neccessity of a conference with a strong focus on emerging writers. While these issues were by no means new they were new to these emerging literary voices, and thus needed to be dealt with in a public forum:

1. What is the role and responsibility of the Black poet in the absence of an organized political struggle in contemporary America?

2. Are we Black poets, or poets who happen to be Black?

3. What is "performance poetry" or "spoken word?" Are these forms of artistic expression diminishing the quality of the written word?

4. What are we doing to develop a strong critical voice for the literature of our generation (beyond the descriptive journalism employed by youth-oriented journals: VIBE, The Source, et al)?

and most importantly:

5. How do we maintain artistic integrity, write what we want (whatever that may be) and still get "paid" (like our white counterparts)?

The discourse around these points began in 1994 between myself and an assortment of talented artists and serious-minded young (and not so young) Black folks, namely Marie Nelson, Rishaunda Ewing, John Ashford, Stacey Lyn Evans, Esther Iverem, Michael Datcher, Jenoyne Adams, Quraysh & Emily Lansana, Dr. Joyce Ann Joyce, Tony Medina, Dr. Joanne Gabbin, Jiton Sharmayne Davidson, Toni Blackman, Carla Peterson, Stacey Shelnut, Irwin Alexis, Haki R. Madhubuti and 360° co-producer Kalamu ya Salaam—my old school counterpart who balanced my urgent idealism with cogent hindsight and history.

Through dialoguing with a wide range of people I was able to formulate a plan that would serve as a genesis for bringing this dream into fruition. In addition, events such as The Furious Flowers Poetry Conference 1995, The National Black Arts Festival 1996, and the Chicago Black Writers Conference 1997, provided much needed inspiration and motivation for the long arduous task of *coming full circle*.

Foreword

Although 360° 1998 is focused more on readings and performances with a few critical panels, it is my hope that it will become a full-fledged conference in the coming years, paving the way for a revitalization of Black Culture and Institutions. The 1998 festival lives in the tradition of two major "performance-oriented" poetry festivals produced in 1972 by writer and theatrician Woodie King: BlackSpirits: A Festival of Black Poets In America; and Forerunner: Black Poets In America. 360° is a complete recognition of this tremendous legacy of what Maulana Karenga called in 1968 *The Rhythmic Reality of Revolution.* Writer and 360° staffer Angela Boykin spoke to this rhythm in her untitled poem:

they
bind wisdom to us
one by one
recording in black
our truths unchangeable
pulling our fears
pushing us forward
together carrying this circle
called struggle
360°
a revolution of Black poetry

The poets in this collection have diverse rhythms, different individual realities, and varied views on "Revolution." What we share in common is our willingness to keep alive the spirit of self-discovery and self-determination which was so brilliantly articulated in the Black Arts era.

This anthology rejects the notion that Black poetry is exclusive to a particular theme or set of specific circumstances (other than how we got here). These poems and poets are representative of three generations of Black Words; of over thirty years of creative "Black Fire." This book is a mapping of where Black poetry has been and where it is headed. The course looks beautiful.

***

I remember, as a ten-year-old, attending an independent Black school in

Foreword

Brooklyn, New York, being told by my father (who was also the principal), that I would *have* to participate in a march across the Brooklyn Bridge with the rest of the school. I naively thought that since I was the principal's son, I could forgo the three-plus hour protest against the racist Koch regime. My hesitation was due mostly to my fear that *they* would open up the bridge as soon as most of us were *trapped* on the middle of the bridge. I just knew that my schoolmates, teachers, people I had seen at The East, and the other walkers, would immediately fall into the Hudson in a Titanic-like death scene. *We're fired up, we can't take no more,* we chanted. As we crossed the bridge into Manhattan, my confidence swelled. It was at that precise moment that the "courageousness" that Amiri Baraka spoke of in his poem of the same name, consumed me and pushed me into a positive direction.

> *...In the 60's there was enough feeling enough emotion*
> *to go round. There was no reason to be square, that's what*
> *we felt. We could do anything, be anything, even free...*

360° reflects that courage: An understanding of where we came from; an appreciation of who we are; and an acceptance of where we are going. We poets are eagerly crossing a literary bridge. Having been taught that we can make history, we are doing it. And that is Revolutionary!

Kwame Alexander
Executive Producer, 360° A Revolution of Black Poets
August, 1998

Kwame Alexander

Kwame Alexander is the founder and CEO of BlackWords, Inc., a book publishing and multi-media company. He is the author of **Just Us: poems and counterpoems, 1986-1995** and the proud father of Nandi Assata Alexander.

Life

for Professor Derrick Bell

This morning
I woke to find
termites
eating away at
my home...
my friends
assured me that
the good
liberal ones
were not involved

Alexander

Our Women

Women
Our Women
not like we own you
like you are the only women for us
it is not the faces
pale w/color we crave
we seek life
our women black/hold onto us
like sunset caressing midnight
like midnight entering sunrise
like sunrise giving birth to daylight
Sista you shine
Sista you mine
not like i own you
like i dig you
my precious black gold
and while it may be counterrevolutionary
you my diamond mine
my mind
mine - dig - you
my woman
our women
black and naturally
smooth and black
and vigorous and black
and practical and black
intellectual and black
and naturally
you fine
our women
dark-soiled earth
seeds planted in you
bring life forth
bring life force
our women black

morning mint-flavored
coffee brown black
copper shining amber
sun-burned black
ochre khaki rust
rising high yellow black
evening coal-sabled
chestnuts roasting black
late night sun-setting
pitch jet black
spadiceous
stramineous
and castaneous
our women black
and naturally
we are your men

Alexander

New School Sketches

1.
in the real world
warriors of the word
don't exist anymore
have become
myopic literary hustlers
who quote Baldwin
while waiting for their agents
to get back to them
still waitin'

2.
without sissies
we become hip ho's
looking for a dick
Weinberg, that is

3.
at best "revolution"
is now a televised cliche used by
soft-drink manufacturers
sneaker executives and
angry poets who don't even read
while machete-armed Hutu rebels
chop off limbs and gouge out eyes
still angry

4.
we write what we like
our words change for nobody
except Time Warner

5.
we ill cause we lack Kujichagulia
but at least we getting paid

6.
i bought my child
a self-publishing kit
when she was five
she is seven now
and sells homemade lemonade
at yard sales
she wants to be a dancer
"and a publisher"
i hope she remembers

7.
in the new world
who will be the memories
firmly etched in our people's future
who of us will represent this new school?
step up young Baraka's
step up young Morrison's
step up young DePillar's
step up young Milner's
step up young Gerima's
step up young Sanchez's
be raw and timeless like them
live by your blackwords
avoid death in white pockets
be the real Renaissance/control your art
that is revolutionary
nurture vision
seek clarity
practice commitment
be the real Renaissance
feeders of the canon
feeders of the children's
memories

Amiri Baraka

Amiri Baraka is a founder of the 60's Black Arts Movement and one of America's most prolific writers. His latest book of poetry is **Funk Lore, New Poems (1984—1995)** (Littoral Books, 1996).

Answers In Progress

Walk through life
beautiful more than anything
stand in the sunlight
walk through life
love all the things
that make you strong be lovers, be anything
for all the people of
earth.

You have brothers
you love each other, change up
and look at the world
now, it's
ours, take it slow
we've long time, a long way
to go,

we have
each other, and the
world,
dont be sorry
walk on out through sunlight life, and know
we're on the go
for love
to open
our lives
to walk
tasting the sunshine
of life.

Fusion Recipe

Take a pinch of
quote R&B

Add a smidgen/ of
quote Jazz

Combine in a very shal
low/ mildly heat

ed/ Crock

of "Uncle Sam" brand
bovine fecal
sauce

Then let the mixture sit
until it turns
to
cheap furniture.

A. Baraka

Class Gas
(for those who nose)

Since the rich eat more
than anybody else
It is reasonable to assume
that they are more full of shit

Oklahoma Enters The Third World

After the bombing,
                    I saw American
                    on television

their faces exiled from
the candy brain-destroying
fraud, fakery & Madness
of their culture.

They did not look like
kewpie dolls of the ads

    their faces were pulling away
from the money-dick slavery
klan sex nazi white
supremacy primitive cave
savage airbrushed, violent
greedy ignorant culture.

the wax faces melted with their
eyes, and they, for a moment, felt
the truth.
And for that moment came
into the world.   & like most
of the rest of us
in the world.

They were actually, crying.

The People's Last Will & Testament

Most peoples' lives
will never really
change. They will never
have much money. Most
of us will always be poor. Most
will never be able to read. We will always
live in a slum. We will always
be in debt. A lot of us will have children that go
to jail. A lot of our children
will be murdered. Most of us
will never have enough
to eat. Most will never
have cars and our clothes
will always be old. Our jobs will be
something we wish we did not have
to do. If we have jobs. Our whole
lives will be overlaid with struggle
oppression, anxiety, ignorance
and frustration. Most will never
even understand Democracy, and certainly
we will never receive it. And this is the way
it will always be, with us,
unless we make Revolution!

Ras Baraka

Ras Baraka, father of a 7 year-old daughter Amandla, is an elementary school teacher, community activist, and an accomplished writer. He appeared on the Fugees album **The Score** and has produced his own CD, **Shorty for Mayor.** He ran for mayor of Newark in 1994 and for councilman in 1998.

Hayes\Tilden (1877)

There is
  no
White picket fence for us
  not
forty acres
  nor
a mule
only lies and tricks
There is no
2.5 kids
a dog
no education
nor recreation
or employment for us
only lies and tricks
There is no protection
no rights
or citizenship for us
only lies and tricks
and NOW WHAT!!

you dropped out of high school
you work your ass off for little or no pay
your daughter is a single mother on welfare (with a job)
Now what you gonna do!
you have more than two kids
and your family aint perfect
and you have loud fights in the streets
in the middle of the night
Now what you gonna do!
you got high blood pressure
your family's been eatin' pork since
before reconstruction
you get drunk and talk loud - point fingers
and listen to the blues

R. Baraka

Now what you gonna do!
your father is a puerto rican
and your grandmother is a Cherokee
you can't speak a lick of the King's english
and all the teachers know about it
Now what you gonna do!
The phone company turned off your phone
they took your cable
shut off your electricity
you have to catch the bus to work
and get docked for being late
someone in your family has AIDS
your mother's friend smokes crack
your uncle got laid off
your brother is in jail
your sister has been afraid of herself
as long as you known her
your cousin thinks someone is hiding in her closet
your teacher classified your child with ADD
you're growin more and more paranoid everyday
and to top it off
you black
you poor
you work hard
and you been livin on the same street in the same neighborhood
for as long as you can remember
Now what you gonna do!
Now what you gonna do!
Now what you gonna do!
You gonna live
you gonna live and fight and move forward
and stop chasing someone else's dreams
and co-starring in their nitemares
don't walk away with your head down
or cry their tears
hold your head high
and sing your sad songs

and scream if you
want to
holler if you can
lose it be emotional
it's the only evidence
of life left
it's the only proof
you're alive
What you gonna do now?
organize
what you gonna do now?
fight
what you gonna do now?
be joyful of who you are
but change where you are....

R. Baraka

Ghetto Tales

you heard the stories about
                    the boy
who dreamed of being a millionaire
and living in style
while his mother stayed on her knees
hoping God a let him live awhile
lost his way at 13
started dealing cocaine
built up his clientele
until he got strong in the game
          forgot about his future
until it finally came
his beginning was his end
          chasing that same spot
his death was foreshadowed two nights ago   so now
he avoids that spot
where the force of the bullets
pushed his cousin against a tree
and him to one knee
          and there's a small
crevice in the sidewalk
where his blood wouldn't wash away
          runnin from the
          voices then whispers
that turn hateful to confusin to know what they say
too many nitemares
no direction
and afraid of losin his fame
trapped inside a ghetto tale
trying desperately to change
but in reality seems like shit
always stays the same
and he thought it was the weed
that was keeping him sane
he tried to stay awake

cause he kept dreaming
about flames
now he was up to four blunts a day
and 3 bottles of gin
death in his thoughts until his mind would spin
he wanted to go out blazin
shootin against the wind
with dark blue tears and
a peaceful grin
he tried to go the distance until the penitentiary
became his hope
a 5 to 10 bid replaced his suicide notes
hanging from loose threads at the end of his own rope
HEY!!
you know the stories
of the boy
who never embraced his pain
whose memories are two blocks
from that tree spot
in the form of a blood stain
who dreamed of making millions but
instead died in the rain....
Now "The Bricks" hold his spirit
and his boys call his name
in the streets
scared and paranoid
knowin they fates is just the same
Yo!!
you know the story about
the boy
who had to do more with less
met a ghost at 13
on one knee with his cousin in his arms
as red rivers flowed from his chest.

Toni Blackman

Toni Blackman, a multi-talented writer/vocalist/actress, is founding director of the Freestyle Union and co-author of ACTCo's theater production *The Hip Hop Nightmares of Jujube Brown*. She is the first hip-hop Artist-in-Residence for the Virginia AIDS Project.

the black woman's struggle

her head
swings
low like
sweets'
chariot

but she
ain't comin'
forth to
carry
you home

she and
her sister
carryin'
too much
as it is

where's daddy?

loving
daddy
meant
sometimes
loving
thin air

Blackman

samplin'

jazzy joints jumpin'
smooth sweet shake
'em up sounds
coming to your
neighborhood
drugstore
soon

folks be fightin'
over beats
screamin' shoutin'
shit like
  this is mine
  this ain't yours

lookin' for the perfect beat
as planets rock
  back and forth and
  back and forth and

Get on the good foot-hey
or is it the left
yeh.

set if off on the left yall
set it off on the right/wrong.

wouldn't even know it was
one nation under a groove
if the funk folks be
gettin' down for the funds of it

it shol' don't feel like a
  family reunion
even though the
O'Jays said OK
Ross trying hard to be the Boss
said/negative/her day long gone
is her day

who she think she be

chain chain chain

rwandan sleep

i fell asleep
on the edge
of my bed
dreaming
about
the face of this
little girl

i swear i've seen
her before
she had big dark
eyes
round & full of an
all too familiar fear

i swear i've seen
her before but
maybe it was
another dream
on another night
when small girls
brown/thin/frightened
didn't spend all
five of their
years on earth
hungry alone
afraid
of being terrorized

Nadir Lasana Bomani

Nadir Lasana Bomani is a New Orleans native and a member of NOMMO Literary Society. The husband/father/writer has work published in **Fertile Ground, Dark Eros, Kente Cloth, Catch The Fire** and **Speak the Truth to the People.**

(untitled)

i have been in debt
since birth when mama put the
phone bill in my name

Bomani

SHOOTING STARS

people called me majesty
said my game was king of the court
papers said i was grant hill
with a jump shot
last season i averaged 24 points
10 dimes and 9 boards
the hornets won the state championship
the ncaa and the nba
was tyin' up
my mama's phone

i was ballin' at the park
when i became a former
basketball star
with a bullet in his back

some muthafucka sprayed
the whole court
tryin' to kill a roach
he had beef with

exterminating dreams
shooting stars

i was suppose to take jordan
off the dribble
win some rings
make him stick that tongue
back in his mouth

my mama is thankful
i am still alive
she says i will always be a king
calls my wheelchair a throne

from where i sit
life is a stand up routine
that ain't that funny

i am a paraplegic
who hates being pushed around
i lift weights
more than i lift my head
the playoffs are on tv
what these legs don't feel
i do.

Bomani

a poem for ruby mae

every time your groans butcher the night
i remember hospitals with white men
who discovered glaucoma
in your eyes
they told you one was lost
but the other one
could be saved
with an operation
you cussed them out that day
"no one will mess with my good eyes,"
you cried.

do you know how good your eyes are
auntie?

they so good
you can't tell a dollar bill from a hundred
or noon from midnight
that's why you sleep all day
& wake up the night
the pain of self pity kisses
your dark brown eyes
both are blind now
you are convinced someone
put a spell on you
convinced that someone
murdered your vision

attached to my voice
are your fading memories
of how i once looked
my beard is full now
you cannot see my river of tears
your prayers wail
you bellow for jesus to resurrect sight
you believe the lord will make a way
somehow
even for those who lie helpless
from wrong decisions made

Roger Bonair-Agard

Roger Bonair-Agard teaches workshops in and around the New York area and has appeared at several performance venues in NYC including Brooklyn Moon, Spy, 13, Pace University, Rutgers University, University of the Streets and the Nuyorican Poets' Cafe where he is the reigning "Fresh Poet of the Year."

daddy

I was glad we met and had that
talk
last year, Daddy.
I was glad I had the chance to be
proud of you
...for something.
For too long I have walked around
  mad as hell
that there was no
  closure
between you and I
asking the questions that only you could answer.

When you were chanting black power in the streets
  did you remember me Daddy?
Did anything remind you painfully
of me, the same way I reminded Mummy of you?
          Of all your children they say
I look most like you.
Mummy says that we both have the same shoulders
  that I talk and walk just like you
  that I laugh just like you
  that when we both sink into chairs
our motions are exactly the same
all down to that
  "world-be-damned-smile" that you have.

When you were hiding out wanted Black Panthers
  shuttling them north of the border -
  did it occur to you that
the revolution had to begin with
black men's commitment
  to their own sons and daughters?
that the revolution had everything to do with breaking the cycle
of fatherless families that make "men" of twelve year olds

and turn street hoodlums into their role models?

Daddy, I've spent years being "the man"
  being the unperturbable pillar of
"nothing bothers me" type of strength
  being a ladies' man
  being an athlete
  being popular
  being funny
  being some other person just to not have to let anyone know that
I missed not having a Daddy around - sometimes.

So now we sit for the first time as men
  and just kick it -
cold beer nestled between our thighs
and the smell of stewed fish bubbling
on the stove
    your voice an eerie facsimile of mine
we are for the first time - relaxed in each other's company
enjoying the details of your storied past
and the whirlwind excitement of mine.
  -you offer explanations I didn't ask for
because now the past is past and
I just want to know
where we can go from here.

    Do you know that I'm still proud of you Daddy?
that I tell people about
what you wrote - that I tell people
that
I am your son
that
my father burnt a university lab down in the 60s
because professors were discriminating against
black students
that
my father is trying to build a university up for

black students.
When you sent me that box of clothes in 1975
with the shoes and the purple dashiki
and the white slacks, I'd beg Mummy to let me
put them on wherever we had to go.
And she bore my questions and pain then
with promises of your return and that
you'd marry each other.

What do you have to do with my life now, Daddy?
          am I poet - because of you?
          am I Rastafari - because of you?
          am I politician - because of you?
  or is it that - because of you I just can't find a reason
to commit to anyone or anything?
You're dropping out of sight again, Daddy
  Please write.
          I have more questions.

...Requiem

Mike just up an' died
Failed lung they said.
  He grew up hard and responsibility
weighed on a weak chest
like fishnets could carry rocks.
          I met his wife last year.
Young and innocent
  looking -
- bore somebody a child that appeared
to be Mike's.
          Young and unemployed and weighted down
newborn, Mike's life
couldn't bear family - his lung
wouldn't stand homily and on the
operating table some of his soul
          just
                    fizzed
                              away...
...air out a punctured tire.

But Mike came back
to the job.
Breathing through one lung and
  walking only half a block before he stopped
to rest, his weary
          twenty-five year old legs;
raspy breathed and coughing up phlegm.

So when one morning
  After two weeks of dust
and lifting
and screaming levels of
some urgent project or the other,
he fell asleep in his favorite chair -
- decided he wouldn't get up again

wouldn't break the smiling
reverie that lulled his one lung
to inexorable, painless rest.
Finally responsibility rolled slowly
over his back - stopped for a moment to respect
his silent lung and
continued like a shiny new marble off him
disappearing into the navy blue night.
Some remembered Mike at 250 lbs.
laughing heartily at some
small kid's challenge to a fist fight.
I remember Mike's spirit
before scalpels and hospitals and disappointment
took it away
Before he died
less of a broken lung   than of crushed and silenced will.

Kysha N. Brown

Kysha N. Brown is co-founder and CEO of Runagate Press. She is a member of the *WordBand* and co-editor (with Kalamu ya Salaam) of **Fertile Ground** and **Speak the Truth to the People.**

when lost, ask for directions

I.
how
can we
end this tale

of two cities
on a map
with a scale surreal
where a few inches
between father and daughter
equal a million miles

with small hands
fingers short
like yours
I could trace
the line of your nose
and know
my own reflection

but these days
we touch
without feeling

I could look
into your eyes
and see myself
but even at our closest
we stand
back to back

II.
each time you left us
for letters
behind
your name
I learned to forget
that I loved you

each time
you returned
wiser of the world
to a household
of unlettered strangers

while you defended
your dissertation
I was bullied
on bus 29

but I guess
that wasn't
the committee's
concern

III.
I am
your failures
and aspirations

can you love
yourself
enough
to know me

can we, daddy
mourn these miles
and
cry
          cry
                    cry
a river
'til we fill
this canyon

and let love
cruise 'cross
on our raft
of reconciliation

nudity

they stood
in the midst of
music and emotion
her cheek against
his bare chest
fingers curled up and
over his shoulders

in a rare moment
she had undressed her soul
and exposed her need
but he did not recognize
her nakedness
and wondered why
she only removed her shoes

fierce spherical woman

in a world
of squares
I spin thirds
entrapped in cubicles
plotting the means
to the arc of my dreams

I come 'round the
bend without fear
of the unseen
'cause you can't be
a woman
'less you can
handle curves

I am
the directness of diameters
dissecting planes of desire
no matter where I be
I want to see
the other possibilities

a body celestial
life light of day
the moon's passion bright
dancing the fidelity
of earth

I am
a fierce spherical
woman bringing love
to the lithosphere

Wanda Coleman

Wanda Coleman is a chronic dreamer. Essays, short stories & poems emerge from her night terror of California life. Her many books include **A War of Eyes & Other Stories** and **Bathwater Wine** (Black Sparrow Press). Coming to maturity between the 1965 Watts riot and the 1992 South Central revolt, she is known for her public readings.

Dreams Without Means

darn things get a might boogerish

lacking realization, dreams are apt to sour
to get bloodshot & baggy-eyed.
they'll stop shaving and neglect their teeth.
they won't go near a shower,
and their feet & armpits will start stinking
up the place, dirt collecting under unclipped nails

they'll quit going to church on Sundays

they'll snore bare funky ass-up
till noon, eat candy bars & drink beer
for breakfast, sit around the house half-dressed
in old blue jeans and raggedy sneakers, smoke
a cancer a day and stew over sleaze magazines
until sunset, crawl the neighborhood
in tore-down coupes after dark, scoping for
trouble. they'll come in drunk or monkeyed up (both)

and slap around the smart ideas

when dreams go bad
they're apt to get mean,
foul-mouthed, violent.

they're apt to turn killer

Single Doom Occupancy

fungi are holding union meetings in
    your urine-stained
mattress. music is the uneven shuffle
    of mules along
slate-gray corridors, followed by
    the pause that
listens to mice munch in the walls.
    speaking frankly
has earned you retirement in neutral
    and a squat
on the sundeck slumped & soap-witted
    in a cushionless
white plastic patio chair, the drool
    on your chin
and vomit on your eyeglasses have
    caked solid,
sunbaked, while your new but unwanted
    tan fails to
conceal liver spots & verrucae. all the
    living you've
hoarded adds up to neglect fostered by
    staff cuts and
unmonitored dosages of awareness-killers.
    the numbness and
tingling between your thighs is the
    result of an
indifferent nursing attendant's failure
    to do her job,
the proper bathing, as is the weeping
    abdominal rash
hidden by your thrift-shop kimono.
    the voices you
hear tearing around in your head
    are those of a

young woman and her lover arguing over
    the wisdom of
bringing children into their bleak
    inner-city realm.
you awaken from your nap to find you
    are still napping
and are startled when the lizards in your lap
    jump toward
your chin and you recognize your tits

Bubble Eyes Declares War

this is the side i am forever on

arms were taken up at Avalon & Manchester
on a school ground two score & five years ago
i am still fighting the absent horde
of fairer-skinned mockers
who would not play with me because i was too dark
who stole my revengeful reports to God
& passed them around
& my writings caused so much disruption &
hurt so many mean little feelings that the
white teacher man had to intercede
to quell the violence, to dab away the angry tear
remove the fists from my hard-pressed head
then when, skirts flying, they had returned
to 4-square and double dutch
he took me aside privately, stared at me
with those great wide gray eyes
then laughed, said i had quite a gift
to keep such papers at home or face
the principal & suspension & that some day,
if i had the conviction & the courage
i'd give something great back to my people

I AIN'T YO EARTHMAMA (2)

pardon me, but you're standing on my stomach

those aren't grapefruit you're squeezing
and certainly not papaya
and niggahplease! don't you dare speak of coconuts

if you must insist that this is a gold rush,
there are planes leaving hourly for South Africa & the Yukon
there's nothing beneath this sternum but
blood vessels rib bone & a significant muscular organ
which gives off no feelings unless malfunctioning

and when
you get tired of syphoning off my sweetwater
and pillaging my salt lakes maybe we might discuss
conservation and recycling

until then
i suggest adventure be omitted from the equation
this ain't the jungle, jim
so quit stickin' your tarzan in my jane

Kamau Daáood

Kamau Daáood, performance poet, educator and community arts activist is a native of Los Angeles. He is the subject of an award-winning documentary film, **Life is a Saxophone** and is co-founder of the World Stage Performance Gallery and the Anansi Writers Workshop in L.A. His latest recording is **Leimert Park** (M.A.M.A. Records).

Poet

(For Bob Kaufman)

his heart is a blue bulletproof vest
New Orleans sufi with a jewish moniker
clutching the fury of silence with pregnant tongue
bouncing up and down like a child that's got to pee
a stone in the mouth of a ten year fast
the alphabet cut up with scissors
in a coffee house of painted shadows
merchant marine starting from infinity
counting stars backwards on a sea of dreams
carving poems with an ink pen on Neptune's back
glowing on the sidewalk in a circle of stares
holding a new language in his mouth with his wisdom teeth
only pronouncing new words when he is alone
and he's always alone
but we know he exists by the tear stained streets
and the neat pile of human dung
on the business section of the newspaper
in the alley near the invisible liqueur store
where they say if you are high enough
you can hear him give poetry readings
about the same time some folks go to church

Daáood

For Paul Robeson

there is something in the voice
solid as the head of john henry sledgehammer polished to a noon day brilliance
there are roots in this voice wrapped around the blue core of earth
a heart decorated with finger paintings
etched by the outstretched hands of the world's hungry children

Paul, speak for us
we that come with calluses,
we that come with scars
bodies shaped and marked by toil
we that hold down the edges of the world with our labor
we who pull and twist and pound and cut
we who push and rub and split and fashion the raw material of this earth

Paul, fight for us
the sunkissed, the sea dweller,
those wrapped in night, those sweating in holes
that do the work that others refuse
we who work with paper and pipes, we make magic and art
we who work with wood and words, we make dreams and miracles
we who fold the clothes, we who lose the fingers, and chart the stars,
and stack the books and bricks
hands full of flowers and sweet herb
shoe covered in mud, hand covered in blood,
we wash the dead and make the bread
and know the sacredness of dishwater
the weak, the hungry, the homeless, the tired, the sick, the lonely
those of us that work
but can't pull jack shit, let alone a jack rabbit out of a hat
smoked booty in the fire of exploitation, meat ass on the hook of industry

Sing to us Paul in a million tongues
about the blood and wind and sun that binds us
about our common struggle, and the abolition of tears

in this voice is courage
pure undefiled testosterone
in the state of service
at the point of sweat
at the place of tears
in the face of tyranny
at the spot of clarity
in defiance of false masters

this voice is deep,
rich eternally backbone strengthened in love,
this thing that grows like flowers and springs from the chest
there is something in this voice
beyond sound beyond time
and it is precious, oh so precious

Daáood

Balm of Gilead

(for Lester Young and Billie Holiday)

she graced him with the title of Prez
he crowned her Lady Day
they stand together on the stage
these cousins of sorts and songs
holy water drawn from the same well
a common bond of knowledge
a raw nerve runs deep
so sensitive to touch
overdose of feeling, life full and aching
gardenia floating on a lake of tears
pork-pie hat flattened by the weight of the world
this friendship sailing in a silver chalice of hemlock
pearl necklace of broken hearts
gold watch of shattered dreams

the saxophone turns sideways
smoke and warm fire oozing lava river
gazelle dance in Kansas City air
Lady Day's angelic satin whining secrets in your ear
the torn edge of raw silk surrounded by rainbows
from light filtered through a whiskey shot glass
the cool sound is pain shackled
and made to walk a straight line, the pure tone of truth

the tongue full of Cupid's arrows
the language an army of bent blue notes at the foot of the ear
there is little money here in this music for the players
only spirit and history
the sweat from hot light, ocean of applause
and the shadows in lonely hotel rooms
the laughter and the smiles of photographs

she graced him with the title of Prez
he crowned her Lady Day
and at the church
Lester laid out in a casket like a saxophone in its case
Billie pleaded to sing, this offering, this final gesture of love
but they, the bloodsuckers, the holders of her cabaret card
spit no on the purest request
shit on her gift and stepped on her heart once again
they carried her off to a saloon to sedate her
in four months she would follow Prez
off of the world stage into the spotlight
seeking the Balm of Gilead
You dig?

D-Knowledge (Derrick I.M. Gilbert)

Derrick I.M. Gilbert (a/k/a D-Knowledge) has a Ph.D. in Sociology from the University of California, Los Angeles. He teaches at UCLA and Loyola Marymount University. His spoken-word CD is **All That And A Bag Of Words**. He is editor of **Catch the Fire—A Cross-Generational Anthology of Contemporary African-American Poetry.**

BUTT...Or The Gluteus Maximus Addictus Poem

A lot of men
Need to go to AA
And not AA as in
Alcoholics Anonymous
But AA as in
Assoholics Anonymous
'Cause a lot of men are straight
Addicted to ass
These are the men that
No matter what
Can't see past a woman's butt
These are the men that will
Hurt their loved ones—for ass
Lose their jobs—for ass
Go broke—for ass
Drop out of school—for ass
Dis' their friends—for ass
And even wreck their cars
While lookin' at ass
(Damn "ass-drunk" drivers)
These are the men that are so
Addicted to ass
That they'll always make
BUTT statements
Like
The woman's personality is wack
BUTTTTTTTTT
She's got much backs
Or
The woman's breath is kinda hummin'
BUTTTTTTTTT
She's gotta plump onion
(Ta-dow)
BUTT/BUTT/BUTT/BUTT
These men are all about

BUTT
So much so that they forget about such things as
Personality/compatibility/spirituality/and metaphysicality
'Cause they're straight assoholics
Only lookin' for ass
And more ass
And much more ass
And
Like I said
They need to take their butts to
Assoholics Anonymous
And cure their dumb asses
BUT?????????????

D-Knowledge

Henna

"On your mark....
Get set...."
Wait
I'm not in this race
I'm not really Black
Uh Uh
I'm not really Black
BLACK
Really Black
This desensitized
Edifice of caramelized
Flesh
Is just an ephemeral
Full-body
Henna tattoo
(You know....Henna:
That brownish-red skin paint you
see on folk like Erykah Badu)
Actually
Last night I snoozed in a crop
Of henna shrubs
Marinating my tropical existence in extra/extra
(Read all about it....in prickly braille)
Virgin olive oil
Splashing my identity with not-too-right
(Out of a plastic tube)
Lime juice
And scraping off my ancestral weeds with
Jagged cowrie shells
Now
I'm Henna and Proud (Say it loud)
Down for the Henna Struggle
100% Henna
Henna centric
Revolutionary Henna Man

And you don't know what the Henna Man goes through
And
(Did I tell you that I'm not really Black....
That this is just a "N-word" tattoo)
And
Can someone get me a glass of Hennessy....please
'Cause in six to eight daze
My henna consciousness will fade
And I'll only be half henna
I'll be a henna mulatto
Or a half (henna) breed
Or a mixed henna
And
Another glass of Henny please
Then
In a week and one fourth
My brittle being will recede
And I'll be a quadroon
Eight hours later
I'll wither into
An octoroon...
I'll be transfixed in an hourly-changing
Racial monsoon
And they'll call me RA
And not R-A-W
Or RA like omnipotent
Egyptian Sun God (Ra)
Naw
I'll just be racially androgynous
RA
Too henna for some
Not henna enough for others
Raw
Finally
In two weak weeks
(I pray)
I'll be back to abnormal

D-Knowledge

For I'll just be
Danglin' slabs of ambiguous skin
Carelessly hangin' onto rickety political bones
Awkwardly searching for the finish line
Of my
Race...
"Go!!!"

Thomas Sayers Ellis

Thomas Sayers Ellis was born and raised in Washington, DC; he co-founded the Dark Room Collective. He earned an MFA from Brown University in 1995, and teaches at Case Western Reserve University and in the Bennington Writers Seminars.

Stretchin' Out

For William 'Bootsy' Collins

The whole
Hard thumb
Followed
By the weight
Of the hand
(all nineteen
Bones and
Then some),
Thrusting
And slapping—
A snake charmer
Taming a snake.
This is the
Way he funks
With you,
Blow by blow
Backwards—part
Under a sheet,
Part out in
The open,
So you can
See what he's
Doing. Not just
Another funky
Bass, not just
Another friendly
Phone fanatic,
But Bootzilla!
The world's
Only
Rhinestone
Rockstar
Monster
Of a doll

Baby. A
Chocolate Star,
He just wants
To satisfy,
Put your booty
To duty,
Make the whole
Joint stand,
Stretch way
Out like a
Rubber band.

BIG FOOT MUSIC (1975)

For Glenn Goins 1954—1978

Nobody
vomits church
basement
like Glenn, his
last supper
was Sunday,

leftover
hamhocks &
cornflakes.
What's so nasty

about funky food,

ashy kneecaps & rusty ankles?
His last bowel
movement was lumpy
gravy,
toilet paper
on a stiff
middle finger.

Testifying is contagious,
upsets the stomach,

constipates. You

See. Jesus
is his
airplane. See

Jesus
is hot grits on
Al Green.
See Richard
Pryor on fire.

Nobody hears as many
Amens as Glenn.

Even here,
in the studio,
the right arm rises

to shield his eyes
as if

he sees something
or someone other
Funks don't.

Please

help him
get rid of some of this.
I know what you

can do.

Lord,

make
him a plate. He
looks queasy,
about to faint.

                If James Brown
could just see
           him now,

giving up food for
   Funk, way down, P
         below D,

                  doing it to death,

   body

              trembling like a witness,
religious as the motion

              of hips.

Mari Evans

Mari Evans is an Indianapolis-based writer, TV and video producer, educator and musician. She is a founding member of the 60's Black Arts Movement and author of the classic collection of poetry, **I Am A Black Woman.** She was recently honored with her photo on an Ugandan domestic stamp.

Liberation Blues

Woke up this morning, feeling sad and blue
I woke up worried, feeling sad and blue
Thinking 'bout my baby
And what he's put me through
Thinking how he done me
How he put me down last night
Thinking how he done me
He didn't do me right

Didn't fix no breakfast, had no appetite
Couldn't eat for thinking
How he hurt my heart last night
Thinking how he done me
He didn't do me right

I get up early in the mornin
Work hard each and every day
I bring home all my money
An yet he play
Ho ho pretty daddy, hurt my heart last night
Thinking how he done me
He didn't do me right

Reached for my work clothes, hangin on the rack
Then I decided I would put them muthus back
Thinking 'bout my baby
How he put me down last night
Thinking how he done me
He didn't do me right

Called and got a reservation
Kiss this house and him goodbye
Got me a reservation

Kiss this house and him goodbye
I don't have to stay and take it
I don't have to stay and cry

Never thought I'd leave him
Never believed the day would come
But this is not the first time
My baby's done the things he's done
Cryin shame the way he done me
All a y'all there last night
Saw the way he done me
He didn't do me right

I'm gone.

M. Evans

URBAN DAWN

He had beat her with his fists and
with his mean meat took her
through the night
Had made her kneel and
          it was all
      one and the same
            Now
                  in the chill
and in the early sun
of this deserted street they
lean into the dawn a
damp dishevĕled duo
She, a sagging anguish
      eyes half closed
hair wild upon his chest
her neck possessed;
His terrible loving arm
a careful choke hold

If There Be Sorrow

If there be sorrow
let it be
for things undone
undreamed
    unrealized
        unattained

to these add one:
love withheld
  restrained

M. Evans

I Am A Black Woman

I am a black woman
the music of my song
some sweet arpeggio of tears
is written in a minor key
and I
can be heard humming in the night
Can be heard
                    humming
in the night

I saw my mate leap screaming to the sea
and I/with these hands/cupped the lifebreath
from my issue in the canebreak
I lost Nat's swinging body in a rain of tears
and heard my son scream all the way from Anzio
for Peace he never knew. . . . I
learned Da Nang and Pork Chop Hill
in anguish
Now my nostrils know the gas
and these trigger tire/d fingers
seek the softness in my warrior's beard

I
am a black woman
tall as a cypress
strong
beyond all definition still
defying place
and time
and circumstance
   assailed
      impervious
         indestructible
Look
  on me and be
renewed

Stacey Lyn Evans

Stacey Lyn Evans has written for television and stage. She authored **Real Soul Food & Other Poetic Recipes** (BlackWords, 1995). She has written an episode of "The Jamie Foxx Show" for the WB Network and has worked as a producer for BET/Starz Entertainment Television. She lives in Los Angeles working in the TV and film industry.

Deaf Jammin'

I want to be deaf
to the dumb lyrics
spewed out of the mouths of babes
seducing us with phat beats
that trick us into the belief
that we're only listening to that cut
cuz the beat is *all that*

i'm not *really* hearing
big boy boast about his conquest
over his buddy's woman
i'm not *really* hearing
sister girl salute the fact
that "although your man is doin' you,
he's really thinkin' 'bout me...."
oh please!

I'm not hearin' it
cuz, the seduction of those clever
little beats are causin' me to compromise
just this one time
cuz, *hey that was my jam back*
in the day, before they sampled it
sampled the hypnotic rhythms
that slowly cause us to
l o s e   o u r   m i n d s

If we were deaf to the music
and heard the lyrics only
we would change the station,
the world even
exercise will power over those
seductive little beats
that cause us to let the lyrical poison
playandplayandplayand play us
Dumb,

S. Evans

diddy
dumbdiddy dumbdiddy dumbdiddy diddydiddy
did he
do her, cuz she let him
did she
do him, cuz he let her
did they
do us, cuz we let them
let 'em coax us into listening
to their lyrical seduction,
seducing us with phat beats that trick
us into the belief that we're only listening
to this madness cuz it's *all that*

Please repeat after me
I, will not,
fall prey, to the simple samples,
slowly seducing me, simply
so I will listen....

Listen, listen, listen, listen
for enrichment
listen, listen, listen,
for exhortation
listen, listen,
for the children
and if you ain't hearing it
then be deaf
no def jammin' to the beat
deaf, to the lyrics luring you to

the destruction of
mind
body
& soul.

peace

HOW DO I KNOW...

The intricacy of a snow flake
the textures and variations of leaves
the unpromised breath I just took
I asked for new friends,
and then I met you
Consider the seasons
Winter turns to Spring w/out a reminder
The birds sweetly serenaded me this morning
The scent of a rose...
                    and you ask me,
                    How do I know there is a God?

S. Evans

Requiem for Tupac Amaru Shakur

2Pac, 2 young, 2 talented
        2 be gone so soon
openly proclaiming the *Thug Life*
Privately seeking peace & direction

2Pac, 2 bad you had 2 live a life
        so turbulent
2Pac against the world
thrown to the streets early
tryin' to find his way down paths
        never traveled before
always down with the Underground
his word is bond
speaking his truth, misunderstood
        outside the ghetto

                Who will cry for the 2Pacs of 2 day?
                Who will pray for the 2Pacs and say
                there's a better way?

All eyez on him
always in the public's eye, yet his beautiful eyes
never saw the true greatness eagerly awaiting him
taken out by a *"Bullet"*
easy to say it could've been *"Gang Related"*
Simply caught up in the evil *"Gridlock'd"* in the fast lane
of a young black man's life

Here 2day, gone 2morrow
2morrow is an eternity....for some
        2 soon for others

real soul food

Don't forget your daily dose of real soul food
Not speaking of the kind that creates an unmistakable
aroma lingering from Ma'dear's tiny kitchen.

Not speaking of the homemade hot water cornbread
that makes your toes curl at the slightest nibble.
Not even the bread pudding that drips of rum and
cinnamon, or the tender collard greens accompanied by a
crispy chicken wing and some baked macaroni and cheese.

The soul food of which I speak won't make you conscious
of your weight or cause your blood pressure to shoot high.
The soul food of which I speak is good to the last drop.

Your daily dose of real soul food should include laughter
on a consistent basis, for it is medicine and healthy for the
soul. Prayer is truly recommended and quite filling.
Love is the most powerful ingredient for it has a flavor all
its own. Your main course is the word of God, for it is food
for the soul. You need a little in the morning, at noon and
at the close of day.

Tasty edibles such as Mama's yellow cake or auntie's
shrimp etouffe are cool in moderation, but you should
indulge until you're bursting at the seams with some
real soul food ... Laughter ... Prayer ... Love ....
God's word.
Bon appétit!

Ruth Forman

Ruth Forman, a Los Angeles-based writer and graduate of UC Berkeley and the USC Film School, is the author of two books of poetry: **We Are The Young Magicians,** and 1998 Pulitzer Prize/National Book Award-nominated **Renaissance**.

Venus' Quilt

You need to be loved
I would do it
be the one to open you like pomegranate
take your fruit between my teeth and tongue
and shine every seed
rub you between my palms until the heat come
and the numbness go away
reach into your hair
weed memories that don't belong
and lay out a welcome mat
for all sunshine

there is water in your eyes I want to travel
there is babies to be born yet and shoes to be sewn

if I could I would quilt you into my life
so you could lay just left of my mother
east of my father north of my sister
into my friend

I am Venus without a lover
fingers with soft nails and need to touch
I might ask you to swim in my memory
I might ask you to make your own
we could sit and watch them like slides

how many women should I be
for you to feel loved
how many men
for you to feel safe
how many daughters
for you to feel pride
and sons to be forever

I will be them all
barrettes and butterflies, tube sox and elbows
first drink of water last toothpaste
I will be your uncle's hand
I will be your aunt's kitchen
I will be your sunset in the morning

I am Venus
cluster of grapes in your mouth and wine coming

we are whispers in the length of the dark
we are cuffs in the folds of the universe
I can button you safe
I can hold you forever
so long as you give me your cloth

The Journey

is a song
black feet protruding the dust covering the water
falling into our souls
the journey is a prayer
find all of us in your song of this world
bringing it closer to where you want it to be
No mind the blood no mind the sweat
babies come and carry on
we do from back when
we do from far forward

The journey did not start from the castles or Middle Passage
it came from us black in the pupil of God's eye
large as the sky and sweet in the humming of the planets
let us carry on
we all pray
the old ones who have been here
the young ones who are not born
we wish to carry your song forward
in all the colors of the earth
if not us who would know blue
who would know the kindness of the sun
who would know green and healing
who would know ice in the waters and fire in the sands
we are the people planted first because we last the longest child
our heart with more depths than Atlantis
we hold the kingdoms lost

pray God we continue singing
pray God we continue the ways of the sticks and the undergrowth beneath our feet
pray God we know the waters
pray God pray God
pray God the journey finds us strong as we ever were as we always were
pray God the children know which way to go
pray God they recognize each other

pray God the little feet have big ones to step in

The journey long the song to guide us
voices on the left on the right
Solomon's song and Isis' song together in chorus
thoughts and hums arms and angles
chests and necks unshackled
never clear from the path
pray God we see how beautiful we are
pray God we recognize each other
pray God we see ourselves in each other's eyes
pray God you are my harmony
and us walking this world together
teaching it peace teaching it peace
because we have known war

Aché Olumba Alegba Akan
Aché Oshume Lucinte Akan
Aché my little ones my coming my gone
Aché let it be Lord let it be
we recognize each other in our journey
hold each other when we fall
keep company when we run
sing when we stumble
blow when we dust
drink when we rain
pray we bring water to this earth
it is so dry Lord it is so dry
and the little elbows paint the land in your smile
and the little feet dance your song unafraid
and the eyes see each other
and the ears hear your words
and the mouths speak love alone
in a crowded country of your children called this world
we the blood of your breath
the skin of your hope
stones of your fury

tears of your pain
hold your heart in our blues
your joy in our dance

Let the journey continue
let us speak the same language in our many tongues
may the path lead us home may the journey lead us home
in faith child let it be
in faith mother let it be
in faith pop pop
in faith sister
brother my brother let it be let it be
we the sky we the laughter of the rivers
we know day we know dawn we know evening
pray we know ourselves
pray I find myself in you
pray I find me in God
then I know where I'm going and feet to get there

The journey long ya'll the journey long
but we got company
pray we find it
know it like our hands
we share
leave it to no one else leave it to no one else
because we took it before time was born
and end it when time is after

Aché little one
Aché

Peter J. Harris

Peter J. Harris is publisher/editor of *The Drumming Between Us: Black Love & Erotic Poetry,* a Los Angeles magazine. His poetry, fiction and personal essays have been published widely since the late 1970s.

A Sense of Ceremony

(A Random Chapter from the Sacred Book for Haunted Lovers)

build a shelter
from slats off the slaveships
bobbing to the surface
of the rivers of memory
(lance the rotten knotholes & cure
 the wooden leftovers with our prayers
 dripping from squeezing eyes of clove)

stitch a comforter
from petals falling
off the rosebush of sacrifice
(drape it over our sanctified bed
 & seal the hems with the grace
 rising from our embroidery)

to keep warm in the nightwinds of withdrawal
pound spring mud & autumn leaves
into a robe without chinks
& toss a salad out of sturdy underwear & overcoats

call the
uncles
aunts
elders
from the cities & the countrysides

call the
Revivals
Sundays
Midnights
from the shade & the highways

brew a drink from spiked hearts
beating within honey dipped pineapples
simmering over the charcoals of enlightenment

mix a liniment from camphor &
bubbling alcohol to knit muscles
ripped in the fiery exertion of meditation

then try a little tenderness
& let the good times roll
into a panorama with a view
from a room with no blues
flirting through the raised windows
with Cha Cha eyes
scanning the indigo skies
& we
you & me
uncles aunts & elders
all wondering what took us so long

to build this place
to stitch this comforter
to toss this salad
to brew this drink
to mix this liniment

then let the good times roll
into a panorama of tenderness
with a view from a room with no blues
flirting through the windows with rhythmic eyes
& scanning hearts flying the indigo skies
on the backs of soft-feathered birds
praising our blueberry walk
& the quiet belonging we feel
in each other's wide nourishing arms

oh but the underbrush must whisper

thick with invisibility to hide us
from all but the lookout owls standing guard
with their lively eyes piercing indigo nights
& their strutting hoots warning against the haints
that stubbornly live against the grain of this groove

we face our fear
by pulling out the book of sacred instructions
for lovers haunted by ghosts murmuring
& sucking their teeth jealously

we turn to the random chapter
on a sense of ceremony
written in one take
by a left handed griot
whose 3-D business card
shows the rising sun on the front
& Rahsaan Kirk blowing a seashell on the back
          in that chapter it advises:

build a shelter from slats off slaveships
bobbing to the surface of the rivers of memory
cure the wood with tears from a squeezing kiss

stitch a comforter from petals
falling off the rosebush of sacrifice
seal the hems with perfume from a sanctified kiss

face the haunted nightwinds with a salad
of sturdy underwear & overcoats
soften autumn leaves with the spring in a flannel kiss

          call the
          uncles
          aunts
          elders
          from the cities & the countrysides

call the
Revivals
Sundays
Midnights
from the shade & the highways

brew a drink from tropical hearts
boiling over simmering enlightenment
drink in one gulp & open your mouth to a scalding kiss

mix a liniment from backwoods alcohol
& fresh water from a graveyard well
rub it over ligaments twitching from a cayenne kiss

then try a little tenderness
& let the good times roll
a sense of ceremony
will be yours to behold

remember

try a little tenderness
& let the good times roll
a sense of ceremony
will be yours to behold

Only Wine

juice from a blackberry squeezed between my teeth
stains the shekeré pulsing between your open legs
sweetens the only wine I ever drink

my face red as when I saw my mother naked for the first and last time
her bra poised in both hands as I barged into her & daddy's room
to say good morning & goodbye
in a high school minute turned eternal moment
her shocked shout & my *"sorry sorry"* an embarrassing echo
that slamming their door has never silenced

poised at your cinnamon crossroads I can hear taboo voices
haunting me when I'm a mouthful of berry away from mothering you
with kiss so distilled it sweetens the only liquor
this son of an alcoholic father will ever drink

I cannot stay sober sipping the blackberry music of our friction
aching in my thirst for liquid seeping from the source of all beatitudes
so hungry for my name spoken in your slurred alphabet
helpless as I spill all over the quilt we become
your massaging fingers dissolving me into your body

blessed be the laughter of lovers for it serrates the edges of the future
bless me with your laughter
blessed be the wine of lovers for it splashes & gives birth to syncopation
bless me with your wine
blessed be the music of lovers for it spices the taste of all creation
bless me with your music

Angela Jackson

Angela Jackson is the author of **And All These Roads Be Luminous: Poems Selected and New,** which was nominated for the National Book Award, and **Dark Legs and Silk Kisses,** winner of the *Chicago Sun Times* Book of the Year—Poetry, 1993 and the Carl Sandburg Award, 1994.

Kinsmen: An Address

I am your mother.
I must tell you
to protect yourself
against women who think of you
as a Thing. A simple, muscular corpus
genuflecting to their whims.
A Black Devil with a pitch
fork they would sell their souls
for and
you your mother's beauty.

Must I remind you?
I am your mother.

There are women who can take
a divining stick
and find water anywhere it hides.
I can take this Black hand
or only the divining end of a
finger
and ease over you all over and
be tender at each place you are
vulnerable.

I live in the land where you live.
I would not exploit your resources
or your failures.

Need I bind you to me?
I am your kinswoman.

What
fevers you have
I have.
What immunities you need
I give you:
transfusions, donations
of organs.
See this skin
for grafting?
We are compatible.
You and I.

Your first food swells and sweetens
in my breasts.
I do not beg
to nourish you.

The Resolution

Willie was drinking Mist and mixing batter
and mistook the Mist for milk.
Didn't intend to make so happy a cake
but that was a pleasurable mistake
of which we partook with sliding smiles.
It was too late to turn back
after one and one-half pounds of butter
after a half-dozen eggs devoted to what
was to come in coconut
and chocolate pecan.

This was our lesson for the New Year:

Be devoted to delight, be bringer
of good cheer, stir as right as you
might, and turn away from no
ingenious serendipity, discard no sleight
of hand, and do the sweetest you can.

Moment

Each moment is infinite and complete.

After you get up to go and I can think of no more reasons
for you to stay that I can say without making it all too plain,
more plain than what is safe later to look at after we have both
had our way with each other and we don't know yet where to go
with each other or even if we want to, we stand out in front
of the house like proper would-be lovers courting
in an earlier century.
I start staring up at the stars because I want to see a falling star,
and you follow because you have far more experience at stargazing
than I. You are quick and see two, but I see none,
only the after-effect of stars in the vicinity of the falling who talk
in coded light after the one goes down, "Yonder he goes; yonder she runs."
This is what I know they say, but you say this is not so
I only think it is
and I say it is so and how do you know
and you say maybe so.
Then you tell me about light, how old it is and how new, how you first
saw time while you sat close by a river that bent; it was then and
it was now is now and it was easier for you to live after that
or was it before
you know it now.
I do too. You have always been standing under this sky with me.
I have always been here somewhere near you.
When you bend down and I arch up, my breasts ending
like starpoints pushing against you,
we make a bow for a moment. You turn your mouth to my cheek and say,
"You are beautiful." Then you kiss me.
I look over my shoulder at all those stars and see you.
"You're beautiful."
Now I say that stars that fall are falling in love.
And what do you say then?

Festival

you have heard
the impassioned question
of pacifists:
what if they gave a war
and nobody
came?

this query's distressed
a-whisper
inverted and the same:
what if you gave
a love
and nobody came?

June Jordan

June Jordan is founding director of the Poetry for the People project and Professor of African American Studies at the University of California at Berkeley. Her many books include **Haruko/Love Poems, Technical Difficulties,** and **I Was Looking at the Ceiling and Then I Saw The Sky.**

Poem Against the Temptations of Ambivalence

Quit?
Save?
Sign Off?
Cancel?
ARE YOU SURE?

ARE YOU SURE?

10/3/97

Poem Of Commitment

April, 1998
dedicated to 3-year-old Antonino Guerra

Because cowards attack
by committee
and others kill with bullets
while some numb by numbers
bleeding the body and the language
of a child

And because as far as I can tell
less than a thousand flowers blooming
means a putrid termination of night jasmine
randomly transporting strangers
into close caress
proximity and sometimes even
more than that
sometimes jasmine startles
the entire sleeping world awake
with lust
for what can't be accounted for
and sometimes even
more than that
a thousand flowers wilted
on a locked-down classroom
windowsill

and sometimes even
more than that
the bleached the monotone
interposition of all regulations
for the changing face of fire

Who would behold the colorings of a cloud
and legislate its shadows
legislate its shine?

Or confront a cataract of rain
and seek to interdict its speed
and suffocate its sound?

Or disappear the trees
behind a nomenclature
no one knows by heart?

Or count the syllables that invoke
the mother of my tongue?

Or say the game goes the way
of the wind

And the wind blows the way
of the ones who make
and break
the rules?

And because as far as I can tell
less than a thousand children
as particular
as dark as pine needle earth at dusk
as pink as the pastel crenelations of a sea-struck shell
as brown as the spread wings of a starling
as Cantonese
Nigerian and Irish
as a thousand words
that violate the law
that violates a kiss beyond
syntactical control
because

Jordan

because
because as far as I can tell
less than a thousand children playing
in the garden of a thousand flowers
means the broken neck
of birds

I commit my body and my language
to the sheltering of any Antonino/Tyrone/Valerie/Yunjong
just about to choose
her own names
for the universe of family and strangers
still not listening
to the good news
of her voice

1998 Mid-Day Philadelphia Haiku

Black men sleep homeless
Freeze far away from Iraq
Still sleeping still men

for Chuck and Jane James
2/16/98

Carolyn Cooley Joyner

Carolyn Cooley Joyner, a Washington, DC poet, is the author of **Experience, Expression, Expansion.** She performs widely in the DC area and is a member of *Collective Voices*, a DC-based poetry ensemble.

They Do Not Have To Nest In Your Hair *

A Tribute to Ron Brown

International blossoms shriveled
as their Harlem roots gave way
to bluster
churned by the hands of bittersweet fortune
on a Croatian hillside.
Global silence squeezed loud shrieks
from stunned hearts—
grieving voices unable
to sound out their sadness.
In the waning light of a moon he had hung,
shiny wet sorrow shimmered
on the face of the world.
As we look toward the sky,
birds of sadness fly overhead,
but we are soon to learn
that they, too, have song—
rich melodies of transformation,
not death,
loving ourselves more, not less,
uplifting life by touching those with dignity loss,
calming strife by building bridges
to peace, opportunity, justice—
soothing harmonies, reminiscent of those delivered
by a man struck down on this day
twenty-eight years ago by an assassin's bullet
that turned our faces toward the sky,
to see the birds of sadness fly, overhead.
But then, just as now,
their song does not allow them
to nest in our hair.

---

* A phrase from the African proverb, *"The birds of sadness may fly over your head, but they do not have to nest in your hair."*

Mother

for Damon

I touch the fire.
Feel
the blue flame,
your darkness,
search for broken pieces
you mislaid
outside
a soul cries its hurt
in delicate silence—
begs you to come home.
The tears of blood
your heart weeps
fall
    in
        mine.

Agapé

Inspired by Mark

Like a full moon in winter,
your light came inside,
plucked blossoms
from swaying flowerbeds
in the heart of my soul,
wove them with yours
in the spirit of the universe.
Before I knew you,
I loved you.
Never asked how this could be,
it was.

Color Of Her

His eyes always find their way to her,
question her face for answers
only her smile can free from doubt.

I watch him throw open his soul,
see him wave his heart
each time he looks.

The glance he gives her
is all I want,
but his eyes are vacant
when he stares at me.
Only those who look like her
are visible to his heart.

Sonia

Her words hang in the air around our heads
like ripened fruit; we hunger for their zest.
We eat their pulp of elevated thought
and travel to the place that is ourselves—
the world of our experience of the world.
We claim reality as ours to keep.
Hers is the smoke that thunders in the skies
of stormy souls, delivering tranquil space,
the spirit that frees pain with so much beauty.

She writes out of herself—each verse a line
from heart and body like a filament
of spider's web that seeks its anchor in
those parts of us intended to live on.
She spins perceptively, extends our lives,
creates out of her what is in us.
Her poems seep into our minds and hearts,
take our thoughts for walks outside of them.

She kisses learning on its face, explains
how you and I must be reborn so that
this earth will not be put to a slow death,
how we must catch the fire and live until—
There is no pomp in words that speak of love
for freedom's peace, that choose the hard-edged truth
over the rhetoric of hopelessness.
She sees her soul elaborate with furs,
in spite of wounds extending into it.
No, hers is not a small, uncertain voice.
It is a voice that lets our own loom large.

Sonia Sanchez , activist, scholar, and acclaimed poet, is the Laura Carnell Professor of English and Women's Studies at Temple University.

Quraysh Ali Lansana

Quraysh Ali Lansana is the author of **southside rain** (BlackWords Poetry Series) and **cockroach children: corner poems and street psalms** (nappyhead press). Quraysh is director of Kuntu Drama, Inc. and is artistic director of the Guild Complex. He lives in Chicago with his wife, Emily, and son, Nile.

give and go

this united center
was outside my backdoor
backyard arena packed
sundays sweaty, swearing

Jabbar stood closer to God
than Moses, i witnessed
gravity turned sideways
by high school brothas

in knee high tube socks.
i collected their moves
like germs on a six year old:
lacey's shake and bake

clifford's turnaround in-yo-face,
dewayne's deadly twenty-footer, and
crazy cousin larry's baby
sky hook, which could never be

released without calling his name.
"Uh-oh, it's Kareem Abdul-Jabbar
with the unstoppable hook shot!"
larry would scream. one thirteen-inch

foot over my head. the big boys
let me hang because of dede,
my sister, who they all liked.
besides, it was my yard and

my goal, even though larry
nailed the hoop too high
on the backboard. i learned
to play big with my squatty body,

and grew to appreciate
the metaphor.

window

a peace offering

yesterday holds no promise
other than learning for today
things may look the same
outside the window/frame
but, wind has rustled the branches
leaves have abandoned our familiar
colours fade to winter pale

peering out, I often see tomorrow
bundled up warm and tight
holding her Mother's hand
she checks both ways
before crossing the street
the snow crunchy beneath her feet
she imagines walking on the moon

unlike television
this glass box captures present moments
fleeting seconds reflective in scope
because we will never be here again
like memory free from hindsight
the pane is in need of repair
there's much work to be done

these words may not be worth
the paper on which they're written
they may not be worth the chasm
that denies our dread lock
but, they represent vision to me
hand extended
window open

the night before tomorrow

for Emily

i have come to a new understanding
since i have come to know you.
understanding anew, i have
come to know you new.
understanding has come since
i have known you i
have come to understanding you since
you i have known to know
you is to come understanding
have i known you to come since understanding?
a new understanding of me has come
since i have come to know you.

crutch

when I was younger,
most of the men I knew were crippled.

some couldn't stand up straight.
some couldn't bend their knees.

others struggled to walk,
as if gravity plotted against them.

in my teens
it was cool to limp.

one leg with purpose,
the other wandered lazily.

I am older now.
the young men move swiftly.

one leg with purpose,
the other stiff and loaded.

I am older now.
my limbs creak remembrance.

uncle lawrence's canes
rest at the stair's bottom.

Toni Asante Lightfoot

Washington, DC native Toni Asante Lightfoot is the author of the collection of verse, **Let Pharoah Go.** She has performed her unique brand of "jazzoetry" throughout the United States and the Caribbean. She is an avid supporter of writers throughout the diaspora and is desperately seeking a new residence in Trinidad.

Haiku World Tour 1994

taken from stories in the Washington Post

haitians don't float
they will soon drown in
what small hope they came in if
we don't let them in

englishman in taiwan
he picks young virgins
giving them the one disease
he's afraid to get

el salvador
donde esta mi
hijo, esposo, dime
o muerte mi

rwanda
dad's hutu but ma's
tutsi I wonder if dad
will kill half of me

bosnia
I hide in a shrine
looking for Allah or God
did they flee or die?

usa
politicians scour
alleys selling doped sound bites
as if they were hope

journalist motto
I report what I see
vision doesn't change my view
your actions do

In Oklahoma

Shards of retribution jut skyward
leaving minds as devastated
as A-bombs once left two cities
forgetting the prophet
who signed his death certificate
speaking of chickens coming home to roost
president screams "cowards"
media drinks the wine of his words
turns Islam into a host of blame
like America didn't train the "brave"
to invade unarmed Grenada
    kill Libyan children
    and leave star-spangled body-bags
    dripping with the blood of our truth-sayers

In Oklahoma
former sufferers of indifference
recognize tragedy struck
blind to tragedy aimed, fired and reloaded
in my neck of this American wilderness everyday
where boys terrorize girls
at a rate of one Oklahoma per hour
where girls neglect children to death
at a rate of one Oklahoma per minute
where guns doped with vengeance kill families
at a rate of one Oklahoma per second
and life creates junkies
at a rate of one Oklahoma per now

the truth may or may not
hurt
but a chicken coming home
kills

Cornucopia Breaks Her Silence

i filed a sexual harassment suit against Zeus.
represented by a lesser god,
the defense successfully painted me as a woman
who showed too much leg,
wore low cut tunics,
wanted to take the easy road
up mount olympus.
afraid of being humanized
none of the goddesses
testified to my character.

pronounced guilty by a jury of Zeus' children
my sentence is to lay on a table like ambrosia.
eternally out of reach,
my flavors grow bitter, my locks coil into a horn.
i am a mute doomed to be desirable and inhuman
to the outstretched hand of a fool

Tantalus
gets all the publicity.
I receive no media deal,
no constellation in the heavens.
the story is always told
as if he is the only one
suffering.

The Wilted Gardenia

for Lady Day

Her beauty was a magic act
  gritting teeth turned into a smile
  cried to be released
  from a contract with misery

Mystery woman carved
  notes from disappointment
  lyrics out of struggle
  blues into lonely microphones

Lady
  laid a mat melodies
  heated sobs by the spoonful
  raped her veins with doped pricks
  nodded into amnesia
  vomited the disrespect
    of playing where you can't eat

She performed the 8th wonder
  made God and heroin dance together
  like mirrors and smoke

Lightfoot

Moses Came Down

The shotgun toting conductor
of the only train built for our people
assured all those who chose to ride
You'll be free or be dead

Last night her spirit came to me
gave me a tour of my gov'ment job
pointed to cubicles
housing the well framed children
of EEOC subsidized share croppers
bringing home less than their forty acres
and a Mercedes
her hymns of redemption woke me
before the alarm sounded

I went to this morning's staff meeting
singing Steal Away
those who wanted freedom joined me
as we marched to where the air
was not conditioned
one negro felt the heat and tried to turn back
I wasn't gonna lose one passenger on this trek
so I pointed my loaded will to his head
cocked my knowledge and explained
Moses came to me last night
told me to go down through our birth land
and tell our people
let pharaoh and his trinkets go

Haki Madhubuti

Haki Madhubuti is a writer, educator and publisher who resides in Chicago. He is a founding member of the 60's Black Arts Movement and has sold over three million books. His latest books of poetry are **GroundWork New And Selected Poems from 1966 — 1996** and **HeartLove: Wedding and Love Poems,** 1998 (Third World Press).

Books as Answer

In recognition of National Black Book Week
(February 23-March 1)

there was only one book in our home
it was briefly read on sundays and
in between the lies & promises of smiling men
who slept with their palms out & pants unzipped.
it was known by us children as *the* sunday book.

rain and books & sun and books to read
in a home where books were as strange as
money and foreign policy discussions
and I alone searched for meaning
where rocks & belts & human storms
disguised themselves as answers, reference and revelation.
and I a young map of what is missing and wrong
in a home empty of books, void of liberating
words dancing as poetry and song,
vacuous of language that reveals pictures of
one's own fields, spirits, cities and defining ideas.
and I without the quiet contemplation that meditative prose demands,
was left free to drink from the garbage cans of riotous imaginations,
was sucked into the poverty of cultural destruction & violent answers.

until
someone, a stranger, a dark skinned woman with natural hair,
in a storefront library laid a book in front of me
and the language looked like me, walked like me,
talked to me, pulled me into its rhythms & stares,
slapped me warmly into its consciousness and read,
rain and books & sun and books,

Madhubuti

we are each other's words & winds
we are each other's breath & smiles,
we are each other's memories & mores,
we build our stories page by page
chapter by chapter, poem by poem, & play by play
to create a life, family, culture, & a civilization
where it will take more than sixty seconds
to tell strangers who you really are,
to tell enemies and lovers your name.

Too Many of our Young are Dying

moments represent a lifetime.

our hearts lose sunshine
when our children cease to smile words
and share with parents their passionate pain.
our children, in the millions,
are dropping from the trees of life too soon,
their innocent hearts & bodies
are forced to navigate within modern madness,
searching for life and love
in the basements of a crippled metropolis,
a disintegrating culture   too soon.

are we not all earth & lakes & sun?
are we not all mamas & babas to their young music?
their lives are not abstracted bragging rights,
we must never stop listening to their stories & songs.

when our children
do not share their young pain
it is a sign of our closed ears & punctured hearts
do not misread the silences in their eyes,
they are seeking sunshine from us
immediately.

Poetry

Poetry will not stop or delay wars, will not erase rape from the landscape,
will not cease murder or eliminate poverty, hunger or
excruciating fear. Poems do not command armies, run
school systems or manage money. Poetry is not
intimately involved in the education of psychologists,
physicians or smiling politicians.

in this universe
the magic   the beauty   the willful art of explaining
the world & you;
the timeless   the unread   the unstoppable fixation
with language & ideas;
the visionary   the satisfiable equalizer screaming for
the vitality of dreams   interrupting false calm
demanding fairness and a new   new world are the
poets and their poems.

Poetry is the wellspring of tradition, the bleeding
connector to yesterdays and the free passport to futures.
Poems bind people to language, link generations to
each other and introduce cultures to cultures.
Poetry, if given the eye and ear, can bring memories,
issue in laughter, rain in beauty and cure ignorance.
Language in the context of the working poem can
raise the mindset of entire civilizations, speak to two
year olds and render some of us wise.

To be touched by living poetry can only make us better people.
The determined force of any age is the poem, old as
ideas and as lifegiving as active lovers. A part of any
answer is in the rhythm of the people; their heartbeat
comes urgently in two universal forms, music and poetry.

for the reader   for the quiet seeker
for the many willing to sacrifice one syllable
mumblings and easy conclusions
poetry
can be that gigantic river
that allows one to recognize
in the circle of fire
the center of life.

MANNAFEST (Vanessa Richards)

Brixton-based and Vancouver-born Vanessa Richards is a writer, performer, workshop facilitator, and student of the Word. She moved to London in 1992 and in 1995, with her creative partner KA'Frique, she founded MANNAFEST. Her writing has appeared in **The Fire People** (Payback Press) and **Bittersweet** (The Women's Press).

Tupac came to me in a dream...

This morning I remembered dreaming,
a six pack of brown bottled Budweiser
laying across a brother's belly.
Culunk, culunk, culunk, CRASH!
The necks were smashed.
The smell of Polo everywhere.
Cylinders were used for
pressing records and chambering bullets.
Expensive cologne became CS gas
and all my dreamy friends were choking
on 2 dollar bills.

Thug's Life shelf life is over
before the sell by date.
Anticipate increased sales
and further debate
about life imitating art or vice versa
or the vices of verse steeped in violence
begging the question,
("Are we
the violated black man endangered
or the violent, dangerous black man
in Big Brothers' plan
of a Nignog cog in a freemason's wheel
going round and round
drugged, bugged and armed?")

Brothers think it's their own free will
to master a failed plan
make 'em think they getting one over
on the man
meantime the man's over him the whole time
pissing in his face
and the minstrel thinks it's champagne.

Finds self-worth singing praise songs
to false gods of brand names.

Living large like a rap star
but you're taking the rap, star
and we all pay penance
for the original sin
of not knowing how or when
to begin loving ourselves again,
unconditionally without the
Babylonian trinkets that shine
like fools gold luring men more
macho than manly,
more terminated than timely,
more divided than divine.
See we need reminding
that divisions are illusionary
diverting our attentions
from the power of our own dreams.

So, rest a while weary son
then go check your homies
while they dream.
Tell them stories
'bout the difference between
dollars and sense,
possessions and values,
which one are best
for(getting)
and which ones best
for(giving).

MANNAFEST (Khefri Cybele Riley)

Hailing from Los Angeles, Khefri Cybele Riley, aka KA'frique, is Producer and Joint Artistic Director of MANNAFEST, an intermedia performance company. She has made recordings in London, Japan, and Germany and continues to dwell in spirit and freakmommadom.

saviouress

finding god
letting go
getting hard
going deep
find your freak
suck the teet
taste the milk
know ya self

holy ground is used for murder and we studder
between justice and surrender

this is a call to arms
raise them and sing your songs

kingdoms come between these thighs
and the heavenly funk shrinks the ignorant
ghetto fabulously

in our ovaries are the keys to another world
i pray for those whose souls have holes
they slippin and sliding through
and meetin my gamma ray
a drop of fallen sun
guns of love

this is a call to arms
raise them and sing your songs
ritualize the mind
and visualize
the queens of the universe rise

after life drum
part 1

dedicated to the inna most

this truth is just passing thru
a tear forms and ripps
refuses to drop
just tears at the drum kit
before a sound is heard

priming the sticks for tapping
moist hands grip the eye
pulls a beat from the insight on tension
suffering precedes the flow
let goooooooo by letting god into your solo

MANNAFEST (Richards & Riley)

(notes for reading: intersperse the following 2 poems by reading both between

We meet each other to discover God

Flipping behind your conscience and mind,
a dialogue with spirits.
Sometimes we hear an echo
and smile upon the familiar.
Wow, it's nice to be really talking.
Cerebral chick satisfied.
Not even tired
though I hardly sleep at all.
We stay up late
communicating.
Dawn arrives to find two people
engaged in the act of understanding
the heart of the matter.
You talk and listen
so good.
The sound of your voice
makes me so ready
to be touched
by the hand of the Almighty
but I want to open myself
to you.
Hear the calling
of my name from your lips.
A message in the guise of temptation.
Just passing through
as messengers are supposed to do.
So let's talk about Faith
and keep me on track.
I will bury the distraction
and suffer to remember
all the good reasons why
I should not see you on your back,
under me smiling,
moving in mysterious ways.
Deep in my heavens
the Creator holds court.
What shall be deemed rightous in this temple?
Divine law is not the law of the land.
Whose judgement do I fear?

and i lost myself

I want to talk to you all the time
I think about you in my meanwhile
which is seemin to grow very quickly
until the next moment
when I am close to you
and we can chill and get high and I
really only want a companion
but its impossible with my travlin
so i have to settle for the couple of days
I had with you / to ourselves /
which was really selfish,
cause I know that all we wanted was
some warmth, so thats cool, but i dont
really feel lonely only
want you next to me
and hear the tone of your voice
which i find so sexy, really comforting,
makes me laugh all the time and then
you sing to me
or whoever
to you
to yourself maybe
but I'll listen and dont want u to stop
and want u to keep on going and I
hear you perfectly well and just
really want you to sing what lyrics i have
just written
or a favorite soul singa of ours,
ours cause the singing of the soul belongs
to earth/
I'm deleerious in your skin/
its hard not to speak the truth
its easier than being with all these
ice ice liking the snow people.
sure, the snow is pretty
but some sand dunes
would be better
to tumble down and blow the bits out my
mouth

Laini Mataka

"Born, raised and mis-educated in B-more, Maryland. I've known incredible depths and even more incredible heights. Like, once I shared the earth with John H. Clarke." Her latest book is **Restoring the Queen** (Black Classic Press).

FORGIVENESS WILL COME, BUT, NOT TODAY

in the goring 20's
people cld hardly walk down the streets of chicago
w/out wonderin if a sicilian-coated bullet
wld interrupt their journey
& drop-kick them into a premature grave.

fast-forwardin into baltimore, 70 years later
my cousin is comin out of a store
& is ambushed by a bullet that caps an end
to his entire assortment of dreams.

to u with the ignorant trigger finger
to u/to whom maat is obviously unknown
what were u usin for thought
the day u robbed a store, jumped into the car
& just shot out of the window, aimlessly
during the getaway.

u just shot out of the window
didnt even note whether it was a man
woman or a child, spasmin against the might
of yr projectile.
u didnt even look to see SURPRISE rip
his body apart, while u & yr make-shift manhood
yee-haa'd towards a karma
that wld tax a lovin God's imagination.

u fool
u rancid mutation of a turd
u deaf, dumb & blind reject from a slime factory
u 20th century, super-bubonic plague infested cretin
u fugitive from sanity & grace
u poor example of pharonic greatness
shittin on itself.

Mataka

u just shot out of the fuckin window!
didnt aim. didnt stare down the sights at someone
u hated to the nth degree
u just shot out of the window
didnt even give him the courtesy
of a contemptuous look.
u cldnt even curse his name as u pulled the trigger
cuz u didnt kno it.
u just shot out of the window
& put a hole in my family, the size of the
grand canyon.

if u hated life so much
why didnt u just pop a cap in yr own butt
& excuse yr way outa here.

the all-consumin awareness
of my ancestors has cursed me
with a luv so unconditionally afrikan
that some of it even has to spill over onto u.

i cant wish u pain/cuz
obviously, that's all u've ever known
i cant wish u were dead
cuz u've never lived.

i wish God wld pry open yr eyes with revelations
so u can salvage some part of yr own worth OR
i wish u an earlier expiration date &
the deliberate absence of the ancestors
at yr arrival into the halls of eternity.

KARMA

all i wanna kno is, did i hurt people?
did i take their luv & smash it against the windows
of their souls? did i violate someone?
did i rape revolutionaries?
did i steal from churches & temples?
WHAT!
cld i have done to deserve meeting u?

was i a wrongful war veteran? did i sell drugs?
did i squeal on nat turner?
was i an overseer? did i make babies with my own children?
WHAT?
cld i ever have done, to deserve meeting u?

did i pimp children? did i willingly sleep with massah tom?
did i help frame garvey?
did i sell blk people to wite people for their pleasure?
did i help guide the goddamn ships in?
WHAT!
cld i possibly have done to deserve meeting u?

THE PERIOD

yes, i have a period.
& it goes where i go.
i do not whisper about it, or call it cute little names to disguise it.

i have a period.
at times, i might even bleed thru my clothes
w/out excusin myself.
i have no problems askin for tampons in a store full of men.

i have a period.
& we've been togetha now for at least 30 yrs.
i dont bother wishin it wld just go away,
cuz the fact that it comes is usually a clear signal
that i am not inhabited.

i have a period.
& if u wanna be with me, u'll just have to accept that
i might ask u to go get tampons for me.
i might ask u to rub my stomach if i have cramps.
i might tell u no, becuz luvin may be too messy

i have a period.
& it does not make me unclean, or too impure
to cook or simply touch anotha human bein.
it does not make me weaker, or dumber, or less than myself.
becuz when i'm on, i am standin in the center of my power.
& anybody who has a problem with that can roll out
& put a period behind that!

A WARNING TO EROS

i'm gonna stalk u like a blessing
hunt u down like a zealous karma
put out an APB throughout the cosmos
and when i finally catch up with u, i'm gonna
happen all over u like sun on the sahara
luv the knots outa yr soul and leave u
feelin like a god on his own holiday.
i'm gonna invade yr senses til they burst in pleasure
at the very sound of my thighs rubbing together when i strut.
i'm gonna braid our pubic hairs together
then work u up one side of heaven and down the otha
no part of u will be left free to claim neglect
and if u haven't turned neophyte by sun-up
i'm gonna use verbs on u that yr dic-tionary will never be able to define.
now. are u gonna cum quietly, or is my tongue gonna have to use force?

Tony Medina

Tony Medina is author of **Emerge & See, No Noose Is Good Noose, Sermons from the Smell of a Carcass Condemned to Begging**, co-editor of the award-winning anthology **In Defense of Mumia**, and an editorial consultant for **Catch the Fire: A Cross Generational Anthology of Contemporary African-American Poetry.**

Harlem to Havana

for Che

what does it take
to pump some blood
through the veins
of a tree
to get the grass
to sing
to spread air
along a river
of dry lungs
what does it take
to share a piece
of bread
to wrap some meat
around some bones
to bend the wind
into violins whispering
goodnight kisses
into the ears
of sleeping children
what does it take
to plant some flowers
into the skulls
of fading corpses
to ensure that backs
do not become launching pads
or stepping stones
what does it take
to extend a hand
to wet desert lips
with tears instead
of sand
what does it take
to fill a baby's belly
with songs

sometime in the summer there's october

—for Staci

though it's summer
i'm thinking of fall,
thinking of fall,
walking in the rain
on my way to you

I

i always liked the fall
walking down the street
in gray light afternoon
the leaves rising up off the curb
falling through the trees
a sunny somber Coltrane melody
rocking back and forth inside my skull

i always liked the way you smiled
sipping hot tea
in warm empty cafes,
windows clouded wet
with the memories
of your poetry

II

in the hospital room
your blinds are shut
so the light won't eat
into your bones

you lie in your bed
folded hairless
in a puddle
of dead skin

your sheets are soaked

in sweat
your pillow full of snot
and tears

and though they carve you up
into a jigsaw puzzle
of your former self
you refuse to sew yourself up
from the world

III

you smile at me
as I clown for you
as I clown for me
unable to swallow
this image of you

IV

what impostors we are:
you in that broken skin
trying to hold your bones
together in its web
of dust and blood

and me trying
to keep
from sobbing
like the night
my grandmother died
in her light blue robe

V

you try to talk,
your smock dangling
off your bones
as your laughter shifts
the light in the room,

the blinds masticating
the sun, and you
forcing out a smile
through the impostor
that traps your soul,
in my eye's spying
examination
of what is now you
there is still
the you
i remember
with quick bright eyes
and attitude
the lips I've touched
the toes my tongue remembers,
that one sunny Sunday
in blue socks
that curled
as we baptized each other
in poetry,
the music
the wooden floor made
against your skin

(how I wanted
 to keep you
 in *that* light)

VI

but here, now,
you are in a dark cell
on death row,
a political prisoner
in Life's endless Kafkaesque nightmare
always absurd and unfair,
playing Russian roulette
with your sanity,

your sense of reality

Death, the final judge
and jury
Death, the governing body
with the power
to absolve
and release
and heal

and Cancer,
the prosecuting attorney,
trying to exhaust you
of your appeals
to live
leaving you with no other option
but to put yourself
in the hands
of bone marrow transplants
and corporate science
and other people's
blood

and though my days
are not as uncertain
as yours
if I could I would
will you them

E. Ethelbert Miller

E. Ethelbert Miller lives in Washington, DC. He is the author of several collections of poetry. Mr. Miller was awarded the 1995 O. B. Hardison Jr. Poetry Prize. In 1996, he received an honorary doctorate of literature from Emory & Henry College. His e-mail address is emiller698@aol.com

tomorrow

tomorrow
i will take the
journey back
sail
the
middle passage

it
would be better
to be packed
like spoons again
than
to continue to
live among
knives and forks

Roy Campanella: January, 1958

Night as dark as the inside
of a catcher's mitt
There are blows I can take
head on and never step back
from. When Jackie made the news
I knew I would have a chance
to play ball in the majors.
Ten years ago I put the number
39 on my back and tonight God
tries to steal home.

A House in Provincetown

where the two streets meet
there is a house where our hands first met
and behind the house there is the water as
beautiful as when I first looked into your eyes
and wanted to swim naked into the rest of you

I remember the snow falling outside
as early as the first days of february
and we found warmth on the floor and I
rested on my back and felt the soft feet of
your hair walk across my chest

another love affair/ another poem

it was afterwards
when we were in the shower
that she said

"you're gonna write a poem about this"

"about what?" i asked

Slave Narratives

(for gayle)

who is to say that your
letters to your lover
your poems
your sweet things
are not the makings of a slave narrative
a personal adventure
a journey to freedom
an account of how you outsmarted the master
how you cooked and cleaned until harriet called
you out the back door
who is to say that
you were not trapped in your own house
where every window faced south and you went to bed
dreaming of canada and divorce

Jessica Care Moore

Jessica Care Moore, a Detroit native, is a poet, playwright, actress and publisher based in Harlem, USA. She is the author of the poetry collection **Words Don't Fit in my Mouth** and founder of Moore Black Press. Moore is currently touring with her band and a one-woman show, *There Are No Asylums for the Real Crazy Women.*

Mirrors

Am I still woman with one breast gone?
Hanging around one man too long
Legs give into knees I can't locate
Was it my spirit I ate when I cooked you dinner?
I try-angles still the mirror is always square
Stare cross-eyed so sometimes I can see 2 of me
Laughing at myself
Crying for no one else
I am looking for the man in me
Trying to figure out why that second syllable
Was attached to my
womb   and

Today my body has no room for visitors, freeloaders or lovers
My frame holds fingerprints from being moved hanged on nails
Displayed on white walls for decoration
I see you looking in me trying to find sanity in vanity
While combing through your hair
I break in pieces just to fuck with you
So you will think of me for seven more years
Even if you're not good looking

I pressed my one breast against the glass
Cut off one arm, bit off my one good bottom lip
And kissed myself the way you did
When I was considered woman
Bearer of children and water
My blood no longer colors the moon
No sperm will find a name
And I notice how woman it must be to feel

Just like a man

October

He kissed October like he'd never met her
somehow he unconsciously skipped over
her special season like it never happened
he could still smell her changing leaves
inside his fingers
fall breath became his breathing air
this is when winter was afraid to snow
she knew several anonymous gigolos
but never disguised in velvet flesh tones
human angels die when spring comes
melt with memories of when you
were always begging for some
sign
were always wishing for nighttime
nursery rhyme
to give you back your childhood
when I was nurturing the man
you fought like an old enemy
there's so many of me
still
how could you love me in pieces?
mistaking my blood for water
today i saw our unborn daughter
riding the A train
she's studying anthropology
hoping to find herself inside
a fortune cookie ghetto fossil
a slip of white paper with red ink messages
hangs from her braided pigtails
she is from a family of whales
or maybe she is a seagull who knows
her daddy was a fish and her mother walked on land
her purse is filled with sand and she never knows the time
all her sentences rhyme
she was born inside a long poem

her tongue moves in a constant state of chanting
she told me to hold your hand without cutting it from your arm
she has your charm
our hellos feel like long good byes
left over lullabies sung in different languages
still suffer from lies and wonder why
i didn't   make we   couldn't be   just friends
you didn't   wake me   wouldn't be   still here

we married fear after divorcing in our first life
I made love to you just because someone needed to
not because I thought you were really gonna love me back
i've never seen you completely naked
my thighs   one eye   two toes your elbow our nose
one raggedy pair of panty hose
half of me covered with your old college t-shirt
we remain in love with the unknown
choosing to never hurt
we are the ancestors of a people
who taught us how to romanticize pain
until it felt like   art
there's so many of you
still why did i love you in pieces?
we look so good together
especially through the eyes of October
she's got my eyes   your legs ten toes our nose

the only time of the year
i remember you loving me whole

Omari's magic star fish

—for Omari Jazz Addae

i'm gonna keep living
until my contradictions die
words change but people don't
flowers grow but ideas don't float
so i am ship wrecked inside my fear
that no one wants truth to be near
just keep the close clear
so we don't get caught cheating on ourselves
i'm trying to find waves in between the streets
i am the one person i've yet to meet
my skin is full of holes   wheat
my spirit is always a summer color
i told you i can sew
i told you so
would you let go of my dreams
don't untie all my seams
seems i need this skin to live out your story line
i need to taste another sip of honey wine
just to make sure it still exists
Omari thinks i should wear my hair in twists
he is a magic star fish
I'm too old to wish   too young to die
that's what a story teller told me yesterday
you're not so wise
your hair's just gray
i know where the sky parts down the middle
honest baby girl giggle
old down south sorceress laugh
will cut your smile in half
if you ain't re-forming your lips
to love me up/down/left/   right
won't ever find balance
cause one is always gonna be bigger than the other
got my eyes from my mother

Moore

bought a new skirt waaaay above my knees
somebody's gonna have to come get me
cause i'm not leaving till free ain't dumb
touch me and your fingers numb
i'm hitch-hiking a joy ride from anyone who knows
where the hell i'm from
burn your tongue like rum gotta straw

dare you to come and get some
keep my window closed
so you can't steal my music

while i'm making it

this life don't seem fair
just want my own little piece of air
living in a box handle with care

so many of us still faking it

souls of my feet are pieces of torn
mud cloth fabric
got a copper penny you can't have it
i'm a traitor spying on myself
my name means wealth
daddy said you betta keep something inside you
nobody can ever buy
i'm gonna keep asking
till some body knows why

i'm gonna keep living
till my contradictions die

Tracie Morris

Tracie Morris is a published writer, songwriter and performer. In addition to her two bands, Morris has worked with many established and cutting edge musicians. Morris is featured on numerous spoken word, jazz and avant garde recordings. She is the 1993 National Haiku Slam Champion and the 1993 NYC Grand Slam Poetry Champion.

beat poet

with all due respect

I'm a beat poet chief
'cause I been around
On my feet from the Brook
to the Boogie Down

My repetition's on a mission
I was on the ground
Jammin' with the old school
since I heard the sound

All this crap dissing Rap
also disses me
Racist writers beat their meat
claptrap the fifties

With the niks and that
bongo-banging history
it was nice
but the uplink is a mystery

Hey, I ain't got no problem
with Ginsberg or Baraka
Allen's cool but damn,
do I have to call him Poppa?

To parenthetically mention
Hip Hop is not proper
Media heralded retro-beat
I had to stop her

'Cause if you 're talking 'bout
influences of the de (la)
look up Chuck, verify with
his pal Flava

(My lineage stem is even
more akin to Fela's
Roots of Ile Ife's tree
I try to savor.)

Back to beat on the street
is where I'm inspired
Props only for old white boys
Please. This is too tired!

Hip Hop poets should go for this?
Yo! Don't even try it!
Mythmaking's reached its saturation
I'm not gonna buy it.

Not a happy darkie who's just
grateful for the parks.
Now you're playing up the poets
Rappers taught you that it works.

Shocked by industry criticism
and get pissed off by our smirks
Pressing urban anthropology
slumming, coming off like jerks.

Fear of a power play
What's going on?
Un-dreadful penners slipped us
hippies and then downplayed the songs

of youth from the boogie hood
out of devil's disco made the good
from the bad, self-righteous inkers
dismissed street beats as a fad

Score of shock waves reverberate
activating spoken word
Reporters reminisce on double times
when the look they like was heard.

I just repeat on the beat
Have to break it on down.
Not leave it to media creeps
who don't give credit to the sound

Pull the sheets off their typewriters
On the records shit is wack
Their olden days mo' better whiter
'Cause unlike mine your beats ain't Black

HARDROCK

for nameless

Young enough
Bitch won't know better.
Don't matter if you come wrong,
Just come strong.

Treat her
like a pit bull
Mean — with a short leash.

Say "I love you" when
her head's weak
and your dick's hard.

Prelude to a Kiss

"Men must love your lips"
he said. Sure do! Long as I
ain't saying nothing.

Abiodun Oyewole

Abiodun Oyewole is a poet/educator. His education in poetry came from his work as one of the Last Poets, of which he is a founding member. The motivation for his work and his life is revolution—"to bring about a change in my lifetime that will benefit Black people here and abroad."

Tags and Labels

Tags and labels nothing but Fables
a gifted child is called disabled
can't tie his shoe
like most people do
but God granted him a gift
to make a gray sky blue
Tags and labels nothing but Fables
they say the black familys
most unstable
the Man is gone
Mothers on drugs
kids hang out in the street
looking up to the thugs
Is this the article in the News
you choose to abuse
those who've been refused
a place in this space
Is this your Taste
Tags and labels nothing but Fables
they keep Black in the back
but we set the table
cook the food cut the wood
make the people feel good
But we should STOP!
cause we've got
better things to do
Me and You
of a darker hue
we got things to do
like pull the trigger on that nigger
throw the bitch in the ditch
any term of unconcern
we need to pull the switch
No more minority
we're a majority

this is the truth of who we are
How can a baby be born illegitimate
Every child is a Star
Single parents who are they
that stay that way
night and day
like no one even plays
with her child
that's not our style
others must share
in the child's welfare
a mother sister brother or some other
relative will give
a hand too as part of the plan
to teach a child to stand
on his own
Parents don't only live at home
Tags and labels nothing but fables
call us culturally deprived
and our Vibes are better than cable
underpriviledged disadvantaged
lower class
prone to be emotional
they say little brains
come with a big Ass
and we've got too much rhythm
to be sociable
there are some who believe this misery
and wrap their days in Pain
or be dumb and numb their brain
or crack up trying to be sane
and not ashamed

BLACK

Black is the Truth
is the substance of light
not a color an emotion
not a statement a devotion
Black is the core of the Earth
the passion of Birth
The Rosetta Stone / The original Madonna
the foundation of all that is
and ever will be our Home
the enchantment of the Mysteries of life
and still Black is a solution
and a Revolution
made gray only by pollution
Black is my Soul
like the depth of the Sea
like the background for the Stars
Black is the unknown
just to give presence to the Light

THE TREE OF LIFE

There is a tree that grows in the middle of the earth;
In the heart of this planet and on this tree,
Beautiful buds blossom into colorful flowers;
And the sun smiles, and the tree grows,
And the clouds shed tears of joy.
And the tree grows, and the wind dances through her arms,
And sings sweet songs in her ears;
And she grows to provide shade over a world scorched in sin.
There is a tree rooted deep in the soil,
Fertilized by the tears from those who've suffered in the sun.
Each leaf tells a story of a world gone by;
And there are initials engraved on the body of the tree,
With hearts of a love that lived and nourished the tree.
There is a tree, the pages of a book,
Written long before even time was defined;
And from this tree, flowers grow,
And birds fly, and love is made.
Beneath the shade and the bark is the skin,
Of the men we created, of the women we worship,
Of the world we live in.

OUR TIME

This is our time to ride the big wave
across the waters and
sing our songs in the wind
to take our land and plant our seeds
and watch our children grow

Our time to challenge the dragon
to cut off his head and place it
at the tip of the earth for all
the universe to see

This is our time to dance in the sun
make love in the shade
and give birth to
the light of the world

Eugene B. Redmond

Eugene B. Redmond, Poet Laureate of East St. Louis, IL, is author of **Drumvoices: The Mission of Afro-American Poetry** (Doubleday, 1976) and seven volumes of verse including **The Eye in the Ceiling** (Harlem River, 1992) which won an American Book Award. He is founding editor of *Drumvoices Review.*

HER BLACK BODY IN LIGHT

her blackbody in light of my need
her blackbody a wound in my eye
her blackbody the braille i rub
          /to know my blinding temperature/
blackbody in light
in special/spatial calibration
fleshglare/flashglow
her body inundate
nightdrum. silence. strumming.
skin
blackboy impaled
penis a scar

poised   /blackbody/   in light as hands in grace
in pricking light
in boomerang light
          /of teeth, of stars/
enameling light
quietlunging light
stealthing light

her *bodyglare.* black.
unanimity of her *severalness*
allah the sum of her parts

Blackwoman: facsimile of god
her body in glowlyre
in storm smiling
sun-fixed, sun-frequent
her blackbody in light
her twist a modification of horror
her sigh a knife in the open wound of want
her blackbody in light

Ina Peabody, Sister-Friend

(In Memoriam)

wherever Ina went there was music...

whether she hopscotched from pigtails
to fairytales

        or flexed her girlish grin
        tinged with a righteously wicked consciousness

whether she stalked her dreams like a Duke Ellington tune

        or savored Life like a gourmet,

Ina, the modest jazzologist,

        carried Bird, Billie & Miles on her tongue
        & volumes of books in her head

moving between the open stacks of love
& the open roads of memory...

Southend sage, balancing libraries & blues,
        Rush City & Athens
        East Boogie & Bougainvillea
        Piggott Street & the Milky Way
        Goosehill & Green Dolphin Street
        Tenth Street Tech & MIT
        Lincoln Park & Cutty Sark

wherever she went the music led & followed

Ina, sister-sophisticate,
tasted Life "Straight—No Chaser,"
feasted on elegance, mental riots,
revolution, thin books with thick characters,
collard greens & limousines, ...

heavy lady, serious sister—even in light weather,

wherever Ina is...there is music...

PARAPOETICS

(For my former students and writing friends in East St. Louis, Illinois)

Poetry is an *applied science:*
Re-wrapped corner rap;
Rootly-eloquented cellular, soulular sermons.

Grit reincarnations of
Lady Day
Bird
& Otis;
Silk songs pitched on 'round and rhythmic rumps;
Carved haloes (for heroes) and asserted maleness;
Sounds and sights of fire-tongues
Leaping from lips of flame-stricken buildings in the night.

Directions: apply poetry as needed.
Envision.
Visualize.
Violate!
Wring minds.
Shout!
Right words.
Rite!!
Cohabitate.
Gestate.
Impregnate your vocabulary.
Dig, a parapoet!

Parenthesis: Replace winter with spring, move Mississippi
to New York, Oberlin (Ohio) to East St. Louis, Harlem
to the summer whitehouse. Carve candles and flintstones
for flashlights.

Carry your poems.
Grit teeth. Bear labor-love pains.
Have twins and triplets.
Fertilize poem-farms with after-birth,
Before birth and dung (rearrange old words);
Study/strike tradition.

Caution to parapoets.
Carry the weight of your own poem.
...it's a *heavy lode.*

DJ Renegade

DJ Renegade/Joel Dias-Porter was born and raised in Pittsburgh, PA. A former nightclub disk jockey, he has lived in Washington, DC for the last 16 years. He works in the WritersCorps program teaching poetry workshops in underserved areas. A runner-up in the 1997 National Poetry Slam, he appears in the movie "Slam."

LANDSCAPE
with black youth

a streetlight shaking
its silver head

brother
spilling
purple
wine

a
gathering
crowd
buzzing
like
flies

the
silence
of
knowing
eyes

petals
falling
off a
wet
black
bough

the
shining
smiles
of
spent
shells

red
sign
staring
stop

malt
liquor
bottles
laughing

y
e
l
l
o
w

t
a
p
e

b
l
o
w
i
n
g

i
n

t
h
e

h
u
n
g
r
y

w
i
n
d

a growing pile
of
fallen

dreams of green

Police officers
nervously scanning
crowd

lights
flashing
like
a
kind
of hope

A
M
B
U
L
A
N
C
E

body
of
swiftly
fading
thoughts

EMT
(kneeling)

S
Q
U
A
D

C
A
R

Police officer
examining
vials of crack

the slickest of
tricksters slipping away

manhole cover

S
Q
U
A
D

C
A
R

the
screeching
smell
of
tire
marks

the unlocked front door

refrigerator

Mason jars
green with pickles
orange with marmalade
purple with some nasty stuff
I never liked

150
BONIFAY ST.
/ APT. 716 /
PGH. PA.
15210

the
hallway
where
we
played
football
when
my
mother
wasn't
home

Ma
cleaning greens in

counter cupboard

me in the back of the
TV with a screwdriver

(my guardian angel

the cranky, old, b+w TV
someone gave us

coffee table

the padded chair
where I learned to read
looking over mama's shoulder

telephone

the exhausted
Thrift store couch

Jeff
coloring
pictures
he
drew
on
the
wall

the window
I shot
the
arrow out
of and
got in
big
trouble

t b
o o
y x

the top bunk I fell out of
in the middle of a scary night

the lazy O of a toy racetrack

Tony the Tiger
(stuffed)

clothes closet bookcase

the salvation of
a sewing machine

the closet where we got
all our hair cut off

the
window
my
mother
called
us
out
of

a baseball game
on the radio's lips

the
messiness
of
my
mother's

d
e
s
k

bible
on the
bed
stand

the window we watched
the fire out back from

the
corner
where
the
monsters
lived

the
smell
of
comet
cleanser

TUB

my
favorite
place
to
read

the
sink
where
I lost
my front
tooth

Renegade

CAN I ASK YOU A QUESTION

(Or will you suck your teeth and ignore me as usual)

What if I asked you
to rest your head on my chest.
Would you answer
or just stare across the room at some plant.
And what if when I asked this
the room was dark except for candles
and Cassandra Wilson was in one corner
singing *You Don't Know What Love Is.*
What if this included a kiss,
not squashed lips, clinking teeth
or wrestling tongues,
but eyes locking,
the pulse quickening between glances.
What if I cradled you and smelled your hair,
holding you closer than the naps on my chest.
What if I took your earlobe between my teeth
and sucked in air slow as a strand of spaghetti,
my breath steaming the mirror of your body.
What if my lips skipped across your collarbone
and up the steps of your neck.
What if my hands were horses
roaming the hills of your hips
and my fingers mischievous
little boys under your blouse.
What if I stepped back, removed my bravado
and piled it at your feet like empty armor,
standing before you
naked as a peeled potato.
What if I pulled back your clothes
like leaves covering an ear of corn
and fingered the fine hair I found there.

Renegade

What if I layed you across the bed
and took my time sipping
drops of wine from your belly.
What if I squeezed your breasts like plums,
would the skin break
and juice run down my hand?
What if I entered you with awe
like a chapel boarded up for years.
What if I was more interested in the twisting
of the plot than in how it ended.
What if amid the bustle
of sweaty flesh and flexing muscle,
I was counting the beats of your heart,
measuring how much air you gasped,
waiting for you to tremble in the middle of a moan,
for a sacred shiver to arch your spine.
And what if all this was simply
so we both could shimmer like a lake
just after the setting of the sun,
curled together in the space between inhale and exhale,
my fingers playing in the hair on your neck,
my whispers washing over your ear,
while the hands of time circle aimlessly
across the body of the clock.

TRIBUTE

These are notes I can't sing, a hole that won't heal,
    tears I refuse to cry.
    splash
This is for William, crawling bloody across
    the basketball court just one block from the crib.
    splash
This is for all my homies outlined in chalk
    on concrete blocks.
    splash
This is for all the brothers who got played
    by the Washington Bullets.
    splash
This is for all those shooters that crapped out
    poisoned by snakeyes.
    splash
This is for all the brothers who weren't
    slick enough, thick enough or quick enough.
    splash
This is for those brothers for whom no flags
    were displayed, no bugles played and no movies made.
    splash
This is for those brothers who found out too late
    that going out like a soldier means never coming back.

Kate Rushin

Kate Rushin is the author of **The Black Back-Ups** (Firebrand Books, 1993). She grew up in Camden, NJ and Lawnside, NJ, an all-Black town with pre-Civil War roots. Rushin has an MFA in Creative Writing from Brown University and is the Director of The Center for African American Studies at Wesleyan University.

ON THE EASTERN SHORE

Moving through Dorchester, Cambridge and Talbot
On the Eastern Shore of Maryland
Here in the land of Harriet Tubman, Our Moses
Here in the land of Frederick Douglass, Our Great Orator
Here in the low, flat land of my mother's father's people
My heart pumps harder, my breath comes quicker

Despite the sports bars, crab joints and strip malls
I can see the wide, wide fields
I can see the swamps before the developers came
I can see just how dark, dark can be
Here next to the Atlantic Ocean, The Drinking Gourd
That same Big Dipper that showed Miss Harriet the way
Shines down on me.

Here, I can understand my grandfather, Poppy
Selling fish and always liking his seafood
He ate fried porgies on one side of his mouth
Spit the bones out the other
Poppy, standing in the middle of the kitchen floor slurping
Down raw oysters long before us bug-eyed, landlocked
South Jersey kids ever heard about anything on the half shell.

(continued next page)

Rushin

Here, there are voices and they speak to me:

Listen now, and don't forget
Whatever it is you're going through
How ever hard you think it is
It's not the Middle Passage
It's not slavery
It's not even walking to Canada

Listen now, and don't forget
You are somebody's freedom
You are somebody's future
You are the Promised Land

A PACIFIST BECOMES MILITANT AND DECLARES WAR

In the old days
I'd see lovers
Strolling and laughing
I'd watch them and smile
And almost let myself wonder
Why I never felt the way they looked

Now I walk down the street with you
And simply because you are always a woman
I get this teetering feeling

Your sudden
Street corner kiss
Accentuates my hesitation
And I realize that in order to care about you
I have to be everything that is in me

Your laughter underscores the
Sick sinking feeling in my stomach and
I know once and for all
If I walk away
Hide from you
I keep on running from myself

Sometimes
When you kiss me on the street
I feel like a sleepwalker
I feel like I just woke up
And I'm standing on a ledge
Twenty-stories high

And I don't know how in the hell I got here
I say to myself

Rushin

I say Fool
Why don't you go home and act right
You don't have to be here
Pretend it never happened
Pretend you never felt a thing
Except maybe in a nightmare
Or maybe it was a salty, half-shell dream

Go home and act right
But what for
I can never go back
To what never was
I can't force myself into
Somebody else's image

And if I love you
Even just a little bit
I have to love the woman that I am
I have to reach down deep inside
I have to stand and show myself
I have to walk in the world
There is never any going back
Only going forward into the next day
And the day after that

Your full-length street corner kiss
Is seasoned with excitement
And rebellion

O.K.
Then I'm a rebel
I'm a crazy colored woman
Declaring war on my old ways
On all my fear
My choking
My cringing
My hesitation

Rushin

I break my fast and admit
That I am hungry
I am hungry to care
To become careless
Careful

So I'm a rebel
Get ready for the insurrection
Get ready for the
Rebellion
Uprising
Riot of my kisses

Kalamu ya Salaam

New Orleans writer Kalamu ya Salaam's latest book is **Speak the Truth to the People,** an anthology of NOMMO Literary Society workshop writers co-edited with Kysha N. Brown. He is the leader of the *WordBand,* a poetry performance ensemble. His latest CD is **My Story, My Song** (AFO Records). He is co-founder/editor of Runagate Press.

No Ordinary Waterfall

(for Gwen Brooks)

may your words: coiled concise, darkly bright, ever flow never erode
nor recede but always be thought seed a growing green that feeds
the spirit thirst of us who sojourn in desert clime seeking
soil deep enough to support dense neo-african roots; gwen
love is you who blew syllabled breaths into politicized psyches,
exhaled stanzaed transmissions which raised our imaginations
buoyed us with the simple leverage of speech booted on the black
rock of conscious lyrics sung precise as talk drum heartbeats
rhythmically sounded by skilled hands rapping life cycles
reverberating off the scarred hides of our time

you are no ordinary waterfall but a sacred pouring sparkling
liquid clear as crystal joy tears in grand motherly eyes
surveying with knowing surprise the accomplishments
of progeny who yesterday were but babbling babes;
gwen, we are the scribes, wordsmiths and versifiers
you inspired, our rhymes succulent juice of precious fruit
grown ripe atop the griot height of mahogany poet trees
and watered by the elixired libation of our sagacious
queen mother humbly uttering a holistic incantation:
write as black as you be and be as black as all we
collected, resurrected, rightly rendered, remembered

There's no big accomplishment in acting white

(after being subjected to some third stream muzak)

1.
if a chamber orchestra / complete
        w/timpany as percussion

plays a pentatonic scale

includes six and one half bars
of flute improvisation

& the tune was composed
by an intelligent moor

does that make it
black
        music?

2.
does a dollop of musical melanin
make orchestral scores
something blood might
want to dance to
or squeeze lover flesh to
or fit to express
what we been through?

is acting
white
really more profound
than afrikan aesthetics?

more tragic more magic
more real more desirous
than soulful us jumping straight up
and being down, head thrown back

wailing into the blue, slightly off their key
but in our tune, bodaciously blowing
like there was no tomorrow

must we really
dot our brown eyes
with fields of blue,
cross all our tee's with the deafening silence
of liberal arts negroes demonstrating
they have arrived by sitting, quiet,
legs crossed and morosely
concentrating on deciphering
well modulated arias
which resist the tapping foot, still
the bobbing head and
reject the shaking of any entranced
body movements other than polite
and discreetly tepid applause
to indicate we're in the pocket?

must we make ourselves
into something our enemies love
to listen to
in order for us and our art
to be considered human?

3.
if one wants to play compose and be respected
as a classical musician why not just do that
and not insist that there is anything culturally black
about such a quest except perhaps our skin
and a few references to our lynched
history delicately thrown in

why not just openly embrace what they do
and be what we've been trained to do
there is nothing prohibiting you

or me or any of we
from acting white

except maybe our individual angst
constantly trying to justify
that there be something real
black about passing
over into the age-old truth
of negro life and history,
abjectly supplicating to white supremacy
with a sambo-colored shibboleth
on our lips: *boss, i may not be quite your color,*
but i've disciplined my black ass to be your kind

4.
acting like our bodies are not us
is one of the most frequent ways
educated blacks manifest
they are cultured

the denial of blackness
is petite bourgeois power

insisting

there is nothing wrong
with disappearing

into the tinkling
quiet

of a well composed

ode

to otherness

snapshot: dawn in dar es salaam

(after touching & being touched by nia recently one morn)

our intimacy is as subtle as the mottled shade of shell colors
on a warm basket of cayenne scented boiled crabs
or, more likely, the faint hint of spearmint tea
silently seeping while your attention is turned
to spreading the beige soft of cashew butter across
the crisp of one slice of toasted sourdough
which innocently rests near the dark
of seeded unsugared strawberry jam freshly smeared
atop the face of the bread's twin – quiet contentment
is morning within our colorful kitchen where we are
as gayly nude as the golden gleam of early light
streaming through our window diagonally impressing
a translucent tattoo onto both the half-sphere of your breast
& the upraised arm of my hand reaching to caress

Sonia Sanchez

Poet. Mother. Activist Professor. National and International lecturer on Black Culture and Literature, Women's Liberation, Peace and Racial Justice. Board member of MADRE. Founding member of the 60's Black Arts Movement and author of 16 books. Her latest book is **Like the Singing Coming Off the Drums** (Beacon Press, 1998).

Poem for Some Women

huh?
   i'm all right
   i say i'm
   all right
what you lookin at?
   i say i'm all right
   doing ok
   i'm i'm i'm still
   writin producin on the radio
   who i fooling
   i'm a little ill now
   just got a little jones
      jones jones jones
      habit habit habit

   took my 7 yr old to
   the crack house with me
   on Thursday
   beautiful girl.
   prettiest little girl
   her momma done ever seen
   took her so she understand
   why i'm late sometimes with
   her breakfast dinner bedtime
   meetings bedtime love.
   Wanted her to know how
   hard it is for me you
   know a single woman
   out here on her own you know
   and so i took her to the
   crack house where this
   man. This dog this
   former friend of mine lived
   wdn't give me no crack
   no action. Even when

i opened my thighs to give him some
again for the umpteenth
time he sd no all
the while looking at
my baby my pretty
little baby. And he
said i want her. i need
a virgin. Yo pussy's
too loose you had
so much traffic up
yo pussy you could
park a truck up there
and still have room
for something else.
And he laughed this long laugh.
And i looked at him and the
stuff he wuz holding in his
hand and you know i cdn't
remember my baby's
name he held the stuff out
to me and i cdn't remember
her birthdate i cdn't remember
my daughter's face. And
i cried as i walked out that door.

What's her name, puddintang
ask me again and i'll tell
you the same thing
cdn't even hear her
screaming my name as he
tore into her pretty little
panties
"prettiest little girl
you ever done seen
prettiest little mama's
baby you done ever seen."

Bought my baby this pretty
little leather jacket off the street
when i went to pick her up Sunday
7 days later i walked right
up to the house opened the
door and saw her sitting
on the floor she sd Momma
where you been? Momma i
called for you all week
Momma Momma Momma they
hurt me something bad i
want to go home. Momma.

Momma's little baby
loves shortening shortening
Momma's little baby
loves shortening bread
put on the jacket
put on the jacket
Momma's little baby
loves shortening bread

When we got home she
wdn't talk to me. She just
sat and stared. Wdn't watch
the t.v. when i turned it on.
When we got home she just
stared at me with her eyes
dog like. Just sat and
looked at me with her eyes til
i had to get outa there
you know.

My baby ran away
from home last week my sweet

little shortening bread ran
away from home last nite and
i dreamed she was dead
i dreamed she was
surrounded by panthers who
tossed her back and forth nibbling
and biting and tearing her up. My little
shortening bread ran away last week
peekaboo i see you and
you and you and you
and you.

This Is Not a Small Voice

This is not a small voice
you hear   this is a large
voice coming out of these cities.
This is the voice of LaTanya.
Kadesha. Shaniqua. This
is the voice of Antoine.
Darryl. Shaquille.
Running over waters
navigating the hallways
of our schools spilling out
on the corners of our cities and
no epitaphs spill out of their river mouths.

This is not a small love
you hear   this is a large
love, a passion for kissing learning
on its face.
This is a love that crowns the feet with hands
that nourishes, conceives, feels the water sails
mends the children,
folds them inside our history where they
toast more than the flesh
where they suck the bones of the alphabet
and spit out closed vowels.
This is a love colored with iron and lace.
This is a love initialed Black Genius.

This is not a small voice
you hear.

Ntozake Shange

Ntozake Shange is a playwright, poet and novelist. Her plays include *for colored girls who have considered suicide/ when the rainbow is enuf, Spell No. 7, A Photograph: Lovers in Motion, Boogie Woogie Landscapes,* and an adaptation of Bertolt Brecht's *Mother Courage and Her Children.*

advice

people keep tellin me to put my feet on the ground
i get mad & scream/ there is no ground
only shit pieces from dogs horses & men who dont live
anywhere/ they tell me think straight & make myself
somethin/ i shout & sigh/ i am a poet/ i write poems/
i make words/ cartwheel & somersault down pages
outta my mouth come visions distilled like bootleg
whiskey/ i am like a radio but i am a channel of my own
i keep sayin i do this/ & people keep askin what am i gonna do/
what in the hell is goin on?

did somebody roll over the library witta atomic truck
did hitler really burn all the books/ its true
nobody in the united states can read or understand
english anymore/ i must have been the last survivor of
a crew from mars/ this is where someone in brown cacky comes
to arrest me & green x-ray lights come outta my eyes & i
can leap over skyscrapers & fly into the night/ i can be
sure no one will find me cuz i am invisible to
ordinary human beings in the u.s.a./ there are no poets
who go to their unemployment officer/ sayin i wanna put
down my profession as 'poet'/ they are sure to send you to
another office/ the one for aid to totally dependent persons/

people keep tellin me these are hard times/ what are you gonna be
doin ten years from now/ what in the hell do you think/ i
am gonna be writin poems/ i will have poems/ inchin up the
walls of the lincoln tunnel/ i am gonna feed my children poems on
rye bread with horseradish/ i am gonna send my mailman off
with a poem for his wagon/ give my doctor a poem for his heart/
i am a poet/ i am not a part-time poet/ i am not an amateur
poet/ i dont even know what that person cd be/ whoever that
is authorizing poetry as an avocation/ is a fraud/
put yr own feet on the ground/ writers dont have to plan
another existence forever to live schizophrenically/ to

be jane doe & medea in one body/
i have had it/ i am not goin to grow up to be somethin else
i am goin to be ol & grey wizened & wise as aunt mamie/
i am gonna write poems til i die & when i have gotten outta
this body i am gonna hang round in the wind & knock over
everybody who got their feet on the ground/ i'ma let you
run wild/ & leave a poem or two with king kong
in his aeroplane to drop pieces of poems
so you all will haveta come together/ just to figure out/
how you got so far away/ so far away from words
however/ did you capture language/ is a free thing.

an invitation to my friends

you have to come with me
to this place where music
is to hear my song some
times i forget & leave my
tune in the corner of the
closet under all the dirty
clothes in this place the
music asks me where i've
been how i've been singin
lately i leave my self in
all the wrong hands with
human beins who think they
can be stars givin off
sunlight while they slink
in sewers & have babies w/out
no african names
                even the children
                are breast fed
i have no illusions that
AM radio will quickly sweep
them toward the 5 & 10 where
they will grow old & gnarled
in the head like that talkative
man who looks after frankenstein
if you were to come with me
to this place where music is
tenderly involved in undoin
our masks i will be able to
smile & answer that i have
no children of my own but
i like small human beins
very much 'n yes i can get
to my house w/out assistance
though one time i forgot
where i lived & made the

taxi-man go round 'n round
the block three times before
i cd identify my dwellin
this place where music always
asks for me i discovered a lot
of other people who talk w/out
mouths who listen to what i say
by watchin my jewelry dance

there is somethin
sacred abt bein invited to bring
yrself to someone's song if you
come w/ me next time music
will ask us both to come into
ourselves 'n be our own children
who forget what we were told
rememberin only to be what we are

in
ourselves
there
is
the
world
& in this place where music stays
you can let yrself in or out
wherever you have to go there
are vehicles available for earthy
poets usually grow beyond the rushes
& when you leave yrself at home
burglars 'n daylight thieves
pounce on you & sell yr skin
at cut-rates on 10th avenue
so come with me to this place
i know where music expects me
& when she finds me
                    i am bathed in the ocean's breath

on becomin successful

'she dont seem afrikan enuf to know bt . . .'
'seeems she's dabblin in ghetto-life . . .'

why dont you go on & integrate a
german-american school in st. louis mo./ 1955/ better yet
why dont ya go on & be a red niggah in a blk school in 1954/
i got it/ try & make one friend at camp in the ozarks in 1957/
crawl thru one a jesse james' caves wit a class of white kids
waitin outside to see the whites of yr eyes/ why dontcha invade
a clique of working-class italians tryin to be protestant in a jewish
community/ & come up a spade/ be a lil too dark/ lips a lil too full/
hair entirely too nappy/ to be beautiful/ be a smart child tryin to be
dumb/ you go meet somebody who wants/ always/ a lil less/ be
cool when yr body says hot & more/ be a mistake in racial integrity/
an error in white folks' most absurd fantasies/ be a blk girl in 1954/
who's not blk enuf to lovinly ignore/ not beautiful enuf to leave
alone/ not smart enuf to move outta the way/ not bitter enuf to die
at a early age/ why dontcha c'mon & live my life for me/ since the
poems aint enuf/ go on & live my life for me/ i didnt want certain
moments at all/ i'd giv em to anybody/

Glenis Redmond Sherer

Glenis Redmond Sherer is the Southeastern Regional Poetry Slams Champion 1998 and National Poetry Slam Finalist. Her work has been published in **Catch The Fire** and *Obsidian: Black Literature in Review.*

IF I AIN'T AFRICAN

If I ain't African

someone tell my heart
to stop beating like a d'jembe drum.

If I ain't African
someone tell my hair
to stop curling up like the continent
it is from.

If I ain't African
someone tell my lips
to stop singing a Yoruban song
someone speak to my hips
tell them their sway
is all wrong.

If I ain't African
how come I know the way home?
Along the Ivory Coast
feel it
in my breast of bones.

If I ain't African
how come my feet do this African dance?
How come every time
I'm in New Orleans - Charleston
I fall into a trance?

If I ain't African how come
I know things I ain't suppose to know
about the middle passage - slavery
feel it deep down
in my soul?

If I ain't African
someone tell their Gods
to stop calling on me,
Obatala, Ellegba, Elleggua,
Yemaya, Oshun
Ogun!

Tell me why I faint
every time
there is a full moon.

If I ain't African
how come I hear
Africa Africa Africa
everywhere I go?
Hear it in my heartbeat
hear it high
hear it low.

If I ain't African
someone tell my soul
to lose this violet flame
someone tell their Gods
to call another name.
someone take this drum beat
out of my heart
someone give my tongue
a new mouth
to part.

If I ain't African
someone tell my feet
to speak to my knees
to send word to my hips
to press a message on my breast
to sing a song
to my lips

to whisper in my ear
If I ain't African
If I ain't African
If I ain't African
PLEASE
tell my eyes
Cause if I ain't African
I ain't livin'
and God knows
I ain't
ALIVE!

Sherer

How do you get yours?

I get mine from a pen
tripping from a rush in my vein.
I get mine
from a sweet drunk of words rolling off my tongue.
I get mine
from a heart cooked over a blue flame.
I get mine
from a tender hand-rolled feeling.
I get mine
from a psychedelic search for meaning.
I get mine
from an ancient acid trip
triggered from an earthly desire
to be rocked, caressed in the sweet night of the womb.
What do you do?
Mine cost me nothing
but a visit to my dark friend.
Look into my eyes,
you can see my heart.
tightly packed smack to the brim.
It will tell you poetry is my wine, my sweet high,
mellow lush, slurred words, slanted eyes, tilted poise.
I drink until drunk, ride until high, nod until I am in the land of...
How about you?
What do you do
when this need rides high,
laps up like grey waves against your shore?

This thing called poetry takes me like a full moon's night.
I declare it is better than Woo Woo,
Sex on the Beach or
Vodka in any mix.
How do you get yours?
I get mine splayed on the page,
then mouth ready to engage

supple phrases drooling bits of metaphor
out of my thick lips
dribbling incessant aliteration oozing
ono * mat * o * pe * ia, ono * mat * o * pe * ia
I don't care if it's not cool.
Don't even care if ain't hip.
Poetry is my drug of choice.
It is my one and only trip.

Nichole L. Shields

Chicago native Nichole L. Shields is the winner of the 1995 and 1997 Gwendolyn Brooks Poetry contests. She is the author of a poetry volume, **One Less Road to Travel.** Ms. Shields is currently working on her forthcoming collection of essays: **Dead Men Don't Vote.**

Happenings

It started
with playful eye rolling
and sweet and sassy sayings

It developed
into an occasional kiss
and a touch and feel
here and there

It transformed into a
stroke of a thigh
and an ever so gentle
caress of the head

And after penetration
things were as they were before

a simple good morning
or good evening
as we passed each other
in the corridor

Sweet But Sassy

He tried
to belittle me
before his friends
by saying

"YOU GOT BIG LIPS"

I said
just as sweet and sassy as a
Louisiana virgin

"How would you know,
you've never been in my panties?!"

MADD

His breath
smelled of
flat beer and stale
pretzels

His eyes
were the color
of a hateful bull's
target

The pores of his skin
released more alcohol
than he consumed

His frail body
shook violently

Perhaps he will see
the little boy crossing
the road a mile ahead

Momma in Red

They said
that the only reason
my momma wore a red
dress to her daddy's funeral
was because she hated him
and was just being sassy

I know she wore it
because it was
the only one she had!

The Crack of Dawn

It's not the crack of dawn
when I roll over
open my eyes and see
not the crack of dawn,
but the crack of your ass
slipping into your pants

And I say damn
but am reminded
that you are indeed
another woman's man

And then,
you frown
and I am embarrassed
after I request the impossible,

That you stay
until the crack of dawn.

Askia M. Touré

Askia M. Touré, poet-visionary, Black Liberation activist, is a founding architect of the Black Arts Movement, and an Africana Studies pioneer. His work is published in numerous anthologies in the United States and internationally in France, Italy, India and China. He is an American Book Award winner.

SNOW WHITE: A REJOINDER

(for The People's Princess)

Diana didn't fit the fixed Anglo role
of "duty," doled out by royal snobs.
Yes, she railed against a dumb,
"air head" image: a royal wimp,
brood mare bowing before frumpy
matriarch. Instead, the tall maiden
rebelled and grew a soul!

Diana isolated, insecure, unloved
among myriad stiff upper lips;
alienated, brooding, suicidal, soon
identified with fellow victims:
the homeless Poor, the Black
Arabs Indians Afrikans. Diana
auctioning her gowns for poverty—
in New York, Paris, Rome—found
joy in the arms of an Arab prince,
and inspiration in the eyes of a tiny
saint. Mother Theresa and tall
Diana united in loving compassion
for the Poor. It seems our princess
found a Mother/Role Model,
and in so doing won the World's
heart: "The People's Princess"
emerging as a dangerous archetype—
perhaps an "Arab" Joan of Arc defying
the British Crown. Once in history
is enough! Calling James Bond
& Her Majesty's Secret Service:
bloody wogs doing an Image Reversal,
sullying the Throne! Goodbye,
Darling; you were a "Candle in
the Wind," defiant Rose.
The poor limey masses took to

Touré

London streets, enraged by silence
at your Martyrdom; called out
the dour Matriarch; filled England
with the power of their love.

Goodbye, Modern Girl; tuned to peace,
compassion, intuitions of the strong.
With outrage and bitter joy, entranced,
we watched the broken-hearted people
embrace your sons, fill their land with
tears and flowers, reaching beyond
Class&Color becoming one Humanity—
despite snobs, assassins, paparazzi stalkers
pimping pain. Diana, the Shy, the Lonely,
became Diana, the Hunted: girl of wounded
dignity, become legend, joining Marian
and Guinivere in the realm of Queens....

TO ADAM SMITH: A REJOINDER

Why are the sable ones companions
to sorrow? Why are their days compacted
with filaments of loss? Only the masters
of destiny are wise enough to ponder these
essential whys. Only the measurers of our
immutable days can frame the proper responses....

We walk these vulnerable ways through bright,
glittery streets
of imperial Metropoles: elegant
slaves of Computer Utopia   cynical, haughty,
morose, self-centered, egotistical chattel
made docile with myriad t.v. ads
by unctuous voices of Caucasian males
gone sexually erect
via escalating sales reports, stock
market buy-outs; and only incidental
is the vigorous thrust into a woman's
soft center
"in the rapid clash/bang
of faceless
Modernity"   these legions of cyborgs,
half man/half machine: and that
machine
          a ringing cash register!

Touré

FURIES: 1992

Why do moderns fear Poetry, or
major transformations blasting
their tranquil moments, their
waning humanity, these sanguine
seasons raining upon innocence?
Who will follow the wind? Who will
don masks of morality, or mask
improbability, allow mundane
skirmishes, when haunted by Bosnia,
Iraq, Vietnam? Boots pounding upon
empty pavements, rhythmic boots echo
myriad fists pounding upon the doors
of our homes: safehouses against mass
insanity reigning upon the maternal,
azure earth. "Sex, Drugs and Rock & Roll!"
was the escapist cry, avoiding real pain
like lynchings of southern Blacks through
untold generations, or unsung Chicanos
hung by capable, Texas hands.
Who will follow the wind, howling
through sanguine seasons, as passions
ignite, uniting battered populations
rising in a crescendo of resistance,
as Los Angeles burns like hordes of
shrieking "witches" in puritan dreams!

NUBIAN DAWN: A GODDESS SMILES

(for Alva Rogers/"Essence" January, 1993)

She stands majestically before us,
a Presence, an Energy, this dark sepia
beauty. Aboriginal African femininity,
crowned with cascades of thick, wooly
hair surrounding the blissful, perfected
face of a Nubian goddess. Her eyes are
closed, yet her spirit is vitally alert,
in touch with the deepest realities.
Her dazzling white teeth sing myriad
pleasures, as though Hetheru herself
commanded one's attention. Such lips,
delicious, natural, lovely minus the usual
artificial gloss. Mask-like earrings
compliment the golden glow of her
bracelets contrasting with the dark
chant of nubile shoulders and ample
breasts. Outlaw beauty, clandestine
rumble of rebel forces, Maroon-like tones
among zombie moans of house-niggerdom.
She is plainly making trouble! Standing
there voluptuous, black and blissful
for all the World to observe and wonder.
And that bright, mysterious smile,
frightening in its Ancestral implications:
like drumtones, shakeres, Yoruba bimbes,
a Black World opens Its ancient arms.
Someone will pay for this outrage, this
affront to the Classical Ideal; just
you wait and see!

FOOTNOTES: *Dash's epic film "Daughters of the Dust". Maroon is from the Spanish cimmaron, which alludes to fugitive slave-rebels, both in the U.S. South and the Caribbean. Shakeres are African percussive instruments, usually composed of a beaded gourd, which makes percussive sounds when shaken. Bimbes are Yoruba religious "parties" or ritual gatherings, where the spirits of the deities or ancestors are invoked by drums and communal chants and dancing. The Classical Ideal alludes to Western (Caucasian) beauty standards derived from the "Classical" Greek culture. Of course, African beauty would be classified*

Quincy Troupe

Winner of two American Book Awards, a Peabody Award, and the title of World Heavyweight Champion Poet, Quincy Troupe was a featured poet on Bill Moyer's *The Power of the Word.* A longtime resident of New York, Troupe now lives in California. His latest book is **Avalanche** (Coffee House Press, 1996).

A RESPONSE TO ALL YOU "ANGRY WHITE MALES"

eye mean please, already, gimme a break, can we agree to disagree
about who stole all them greenbacks from all them S & Ls,
owns all the major corporations in red white & blue america, who
closed all those military bases,
fired all you "angry white males" in the first place, who
was it, some out-of-work black jigaboo, some poor illegal immigrant
who stole what job from who, or was it your good-old-boy neighbor who
looks just like you that broke your balls - no foolin? - calls himself buddy

tell me, who runs all the big banks & movie studios in this country, who
owns all the powerful daily newspapers, writes most of the major stories,
shoots us with all this song & dance rapid fire over god's airwaves,
who sits on benches in judgement of everybody, who
brings most of the dope that destroys our children
into this country, who planted the hatred in the KKK, the white aryan nation
in the first place, who sent all those jews to ovens back in world war two,
who wins the title hands down for being the champion serial killer
on the planet, who lynched all those black & american indian people
just because they could, who's polluting, destroying the ecology of the planet
just for money & property, who wiped out all those american plains indians,
gave them all those doctored-up blankets laced with disease,
who bloomed a mushroom cloud over nagasaki & hiroshima, who
unleashed AIDS in central africa, gave us tarzan as king of the jungle,
like elvis got to be the "king of rock 'n' roll" after he chained all those black
blues singers to his voice, who complains all the time about this or that
about not getting a fair shake if things don't go their way,
like a petulant two-year-old with their mouth stuck out in a pout,
wearing some cheapo rug toupee on their shiny, bald pates, who do

you do, white boys, that's who, eye mean, is it anybody's fault you can't sky
walk like MJ through space, what do you want, for christ's sake, everything
you done created, all the test-tube heroes as white boys in the first place —
batman, superman, spiderman, john wayne, indiana jones—
inside your own media laboratories

eye mean, whose fault is it you don't believe you've got any flesh-
&-blood "real" live heroes anymore—do tell, shut my mouth wide open—
walking on the planet, eye mean, is that my fault, too

what's the problem here, when you can go right out & make a hero up,
invent all the ones you like with a flick of a TV teleprompter, movie camera
switch &, voilà,
there you are, all of a sudden you've got a short sylvester
stallone invented bigger to idolize & immortalize forever
as "rocky" through "tricknology"—which elijah muhammad told us once
was your game—who beats up on any man twice his size that comes along,
but especially large black men, when everybody & their mama knows
white men haven't had a real great boxing champion for years,
& you talking about being disadvantaged in everything
because of affirmative action, which you've had all along in the first place,
talking about some myth of a level playing field that's been tilted now
to favor me when everyone & their mama knows
it's been tilted all along to favor you, anyhow,
go tell that simple-simon bullshit to someone else

"eenie meanie minie moe, catch a nigga by his toe, if he hollers let him go,
eenie meanie minie moe"

eye mean, please, gimme a break already
eye can't take too much more of this bullshit

eye mean

who bankrupted orange county, passed proposition thirteen—
now all you guys don't speak at once answering these tough, complicated
questions, please, take your time, get it right—who invented computers,
creating all the paper-pushing service empires
that put all you rust-belt blue-collar "angry white male" workers—
& black & brown & yellow & red & female workers, too — out of work
in the first place, though "those people" are not entitled to anger
because they don't count in america these days

Troupe

now let's see, was it "eenie meanie minie moe"
who let the genie out his bottle so he could grow some more into, say,
a jigaboo-niggra-scalawag, who took the whole nine yards & everything else
that wasn't tied down, maybe it was some indian chief, sioux perhaps,
some ghost returned from the grave disguised as sitting bull,
or a ching-chong-slick charlie-chan chinaman
& his nefarious gang of thieves, maybe a mexican "wetback" perhaps,
or some inscrutable slant-eyed japanese kamikaze businessman
who took away all your sweat, all your life savings, but it wasn't buddy,
no, it couldn't have been buddy, your next-door neighbor,
who looks just like you, & is you,
could it,
was it— eye mean, who lied about just about everything imaginable
in this century, & before this century, anyway, back in time to whenever
christopher columbus lied about discovering america—he didn't
because you can't discover anything that was already here
& accounted for in the first place—so please, get serious
for once, give me a break, will ya, just cool it, lighten up
don't be so uptight, go out & get yourselves a good lay, grow up

the world isn't going to continue to be your own private
oyster bed for only you to feed on anymore, you two-year-old
spoiled brat
get a move on, "straighten up & fly right"
stop all your goddamn complaining & whining
just shut the fuck up, will ya

just shut the fuck up

POEM FOR MY FATHER

for Quincy T. Trouppe, Sr.

father, it was an honor to be there, in the dugout with you
the glory of great black men swinging their lives as bats
at tiny white balls burning in at unbelievable speeds
riding up & in & out
a curve breaking down wicked, like a ball falling off a high table
moving away, snaking down, screwing its stitched magic
into chitling circuit air, its comma seams spinning
toward breakdown, dipping, like a hipster
bebopping a knee-dip strike in the charlie parker forties
wrist curling, like a swan's neck
behind a slick black back
cupping an invisible ball of dreams
& you there, father, regal as african obeah man
sculpted out of wood, from a sacred tree of no name no place origin
thick roots branding down into cherokee & someplace else lost
way back in africa, the sap running dry crossing
from north carolina into georgia, inside grandmother mary's womb
who was your mother & had you there in the violence of that red soil
ink blotter news gone now into blood & bone graves
of american blues, sponging rococo
truth long gone as dinosaurs
the agent-oranged landscape of former names
absent of african polysyllables, dry husk consonants there now
in their place, names flat as polluted rivers
& that guitar string smile always snaking across
some virulent american redneck's face
scorching, like atomic heat, mushrooming over nagasaki
& hiroshima, the fever-blistered shadows of it all
inked, as body etchings, into sizzled concrete
but you there, father, through it all, a yardbird solo
riffing on bat & ball glory, breaking down all fabricated myths
of white major-league legends, of who was better than who
beating them at their own crap games with killer bats
as bud powell swung his silence into beauty

of a josh gibson home run skittering across piano keys of bleachers
shattering all manufactured legends up there in lights, struck out
white knights on the risky slippery edge of amazement
awe, the miraculous truth slipping through
steeped & disguised in the blues, confluencing
like the point at the cross
when a fastball hides itself up in a shimmying slider
curve breaking down & away in a wicked sly grin
curved & broken-down like the back of an ass-scratching uncle tom
who like old satchel paige delivering his famed hesitation pitch
before coming back with a high hard fast one, rising
is sometimes slicker, slipping & sliding
& quicker than a professional hitman
the deadliness of it all, the sudden strike
like that of the brown bomber's short crossing right
or the hook of sugar ray robinson's lightning cobra bite

& you there father through it all, catching rhythms of chono
pozo balls, drumming like cuban conga beats into your catcher's mitt
hand & fast as cool papa bell jumping into bed
before the lights went out

of the old negro baseball league, a promise you were
father, a harbinger, of shock waves, soon come

wadud is a Philadelphia-based poet/musician. His debut CD is **no additives or preservatives** (SOSA Records). He is a member of Jamaaladeen Tacuma's band, Brother Zone, and performs regularly throughout Europe.

Hardcore

This is for all those supposed hardcore hip-hoppers
hoppin' round on one leg in the wrong direction
bein' spoon fed the notion
that Blk on Blk crime is somehow sexy
that if you look like you can kill somebody
u ain't got to be able to do it
but if u look like you can kill somebody
then you all that

imitation base sounds destroy
blk boy creativity
turn em into pistol whippas
of family members and
there is no deeper meaning.
imaginary talent recycles young folk
over and over
with a hip-hope life span of
2.34 records
booooooom bip

but him was real bop
on the cover of rap weekly
baldheaded with a snarl of spit
hanging from his lower lip
financially secure
synthetically angry
his job was to keep blk boys pointed
toward prison.
so him dressed like convict
or at least him was told to dress like convict
cause that's what sold records
incarcerated clothing
droopy jeans
oversize backwardness
with draws showin' IQ sizes
and learned symbols of power

wadud

strapped to the front of his pelvis
him said:
Let me hear the ladies make some noise
some body say AAAAL-aaw yeah

they said you be sexy if you hardcore
if you could stroke a girl while
drinkin' a 40
bus' a cap in her temple
while stabn' yo' brother
in a video dream.
put a gat in yo' mouf foo'

so he called himself sexy man
bigdaddy allpenis
da' mac machine
moneymaker g-love u too much
bitchnigga afrikan.

him wore a medallion with
misspelled words
a cold-blooded x curl commercial
for young people to follow
and white folk to exploit
he had a chain saw in the projects
like a blk gimmick with no trees to cut
the negro rapper boy who wanted the world
to believe him out of his mind
so he get respect from other people
who beeeeezzzzzzz stupid
but u see
the SOURCE of hip-hop flows from
the pockets of white folks
tellin' us what they'll spend their money on
and what they won't:

ok lil' blk boys

we'll pay for images
of anger and lack of self-control,
so when we split
some of your baldheaded skulls
we'll be able to justify it.
now stand over there wit' this
beer bottle and gun in yo' hand
and say "cheese"
so america's most wanted posters
can match your album cover.

u see
when u own the circus
when u come out the pocket
and pay for the circus
the clowns have to dress the way u
want them to dress
or they can't perform.

no other group of people
would allow their children's images
to be portrayed as
something so insignificant.

death row is da' label dat' pays me . . .
watch the trick

u can dance now

wadud

3003

the year 3003
black people are two shades lighter
and predominantly Republican
the best selling album is
by public friend #1
entitled "Scared of a mulatto planet"

the middle class/has really moved
in the middle
while African Americans
sit up underneath
the front of the bus
satisfied
but holdin' on tight

six white people
still wait for a blue-eyed hippie
nicknamed Christ to come again
still waitin'

a japanese homosexual was elected president
of the U.S.
beatin out Jesse by two votes
run Jesse run

Israel/need to expand
because three more people
became Jews
occupying Africa
All the middle east
and jamaica just in case

the ozone came and gone twice
water has evaporated
American Indians sold as antiques
while air is on sale for $3.50 a breath

children are raising their parents
the homeless/hell yeah/still homeless
while the projects have been renamed
minimum security holding facilities

teenage pregnancy is required
abortion is mandatory
while cross-dressing is the fashion of the time

the price of gold is up
South Africans are free
to do absolutely nothing
as the revolution revolves

Congress passed a bill
making morals illegal
education is cheap
drugs are free
while God
my God
G.O.D.
has been banned in thirty-two states
moving forward
as we head into the future
blind-folded
on roller skates
making progress

3003
Can I get a witness?

Afaa Michael Weaver

Afaa Michael Weaver, formerly known as Michael S. Weaver, is a veteran of fifteen years as a blue-collar factory worker in his native Baltimore. **Talismans** is his sixth book of poetry. Weaver's new play is *Candydips & Hallelujah.* He is Alumnae Professor of English at Simmons College in Boston.

The Poets

1965-1968

In the gymnasium the balls spun
from their fingers like spiders' silk,
fine and unconquerable. Legs woven
in threads of hope, they jumped,
came down on silent sneakers,
dashing any hopes we had of winning.
They were the blacks, the black blacks
who had the advantage of being born.

Dunbar, the high school that sent
a jingle in a broken tongue to colleges
on full scholarships. Dunbar, the high
school that we watched march here
to smash us once again, we black boys
with all these white boys too thick
to dance like a knife in the air,
to open, cut, slice a tangled history.

Breath held back "nigger" in the air
over the bleachers. Breath held back
"wino junkies" under the old clock
over the hollering wooden floor where
we sang pep songs in German, peeping
inside our shirts and ties at our own
magic. The Dunbar Poets made baskets
while strolling, dreaming of rivers.

"Coach, we can't do nothing with
these darkies from Dunbar. Coach,
their bodies ain't bodies. They are
songs from somewhere unfair to us."
We, the black folk at Polytechnic,
wished from the white sea of equality

that Dunbar would stamp blackness
all over this stiff building to save us.

The lead opened so wide it was
too hard for The Poets to keep from
laughing. They slapped their hands
and did the slow jazz of black boys
walking away from an easy game.
In the streets, we watched them stride
away in Florsheims to get high,
too brilliant to live, too brilliant to die.

Mama's Hoodlum

The summer
out of high school
I started drinking and
hanging out with tough boys.
I carried a knife cause
we didn't bother much
with guns. The older, tougher
men had Roscoes of
various calibers. I drank
Thunderbird and Pineapple Richard's
cause they was less than
a dollar for a whole fifth.
The next day your head felt
like it was slapped against
the Grand Canyon. We raced
my father's car and almost
killed ourselves quite a few times.
We threatened people
and was generally thought
to be a gang. We was Big Time
in Baltimore. Some of my boys
shot up heroin and smoked reefer.
One night I got so high
my friends dumped me on my porch.
Mama opened the door,
and I fell into the living room,
rolling around like a seal.
I was wrestling with my manhood.
Mama went for my wallet,
and I stood up as if to hit her.
Daddy jumped up like Joe Louis,
and I was bout to cry but I broke
for the back door and disappeared.
Daddy tried to follow me
in his car I used for racing,

but I hid in a friend's house.
Then I jumped in a cab and
went to Danny's house, where
I slept. Danny's father was
the president of Coppin State College.
Cousin Geff brought me home
the next day after I called
from Uncle Geth's to apologize.
There was nothing like being high,
feeling brave, having the respect
of other boys who swore to die for me.
"Mike, man, I would go down for you."
Music like *Junior Walker and the All-Stars*
playing, "I'm a roadrunner, Baby.
Can't stay in one place too long,"
while I raced city streets at seventy
miles per hour in summer time.
Being bad felt so good and right
while Mama sat home and worried
about how and when I might die.

The Incomplete Heart

When my son was born retarded,
Mama forgot she had begged me
to get an abortion and send this boy
back to God. He had Down's Syndrome,
complete with a heart that was without
a wall between the lower chambers.
His blood ran through his body
without proper direction, like love.
One morning he did not wake up,
after the daily rushes to the hospital,
after ten months of trying to live,
of smiling when I tickled him but
not being able to sit up or develop.
I went with my wife to a department store
to buy his funeral outfit. We was just
children our damn selves, just children,
and we had to bury this first son
we had named a junior. At the funeral,
his mother tried to take him out
of the casket, and we had to pull
her back and make her sit down.
Girl, let the dead go, let him go.

I cried a little but mostly was a man,
until a year later when I drove
through the city, chased by police
at high speed from the cemetery.
I was on the television and everything.
They had me in chains, and I crawled
over to Mama and cried on her knees.
I had gone insane. I wanted to forget
the power was given to God,
who had took my son and my mind.

360° is only a beginning!

360°, like much of Black life, was done on a moment's notice. Opportunity presented itself. We seized the time.

360° is Kwame Alexander's idea. He started with the premise of getting a bunch of emerging twenty-something Black poets together with a few fifty-plus old headz. Later, Kwame invited me to participate as a consultant. Together we broadened the focus slightly and came up with the present concept: a reading, an anthology, a recording, an internet broadcast, and a video.

360°, the book, is a lil' taste of what's up recently with people-oriented, politically motivated Black poetry. Had we more time and resources the selection of poets would certainly have been more extensive than the quick handful of dynamitely delightful wordsmiths word-slinging through here.

Even though it would be safe to wager that a good number of these poets are writers you've not heard or read before, their unfamiliarity is not simply because they are so-called "young" and "emerging"—well over half of the assembled poets have been at their craft for a decade or more. The reason many of these writers are relatively unknown is because there are very few Black-controlled literary magazines and journals available to connect our poets with our people.

"Back in the day" (in the late sixties and early seventies) we had *Negro Digest/Black World, The Journal of Black Poetry, Black Dialogue, Black Books Bulletin, Black Scholar, Soul Book,* and dozens of regional literary publications. None of them were housed on predominantely White college campuses, and, with the exception of *Negro Digest/Black World* (a Johnson publication), all of them were community-based and community-oriented. This meant that people-oriented poetry was heard, read, widely disseminated and broadly discussed throughout the Black community. What do we have today?

Because Black people don't control the publication of Black poetry, we decided to do an anthology in conjunction with the 360° event. We owe our ancestors the commitment of carrying on our vibrant and vital literary tradition. We owe our future progeny the legacy of documenting what we are doing today. We owe ourselves the self-respect of not waiting for or begging/soliciting others to publish our work and, thereby, allowing others to determine both the quality and published quantity of our literature. This anthology impressively fills a gaping Black poetry publishing void. When was the last time you read an anthology of Black poetry containing many of the major Black poets of its time which was edited and published by Blacks? Don't hurt yourself thinking about it, it was decades ago!

Even though we had less than three months to put together an anthology that would otherwise take a year or more, and regardless of our incompleteness (for various reasons we were unable to get some poets we really wanted to include) and regardless of our bias (for various reasons we chose not to include some poets we could have gotten), we are very proud of 360° .

***

360° is a fierce book. We are serious about ourselves and the whole world. We are not romantics. We are as critical of our own shortcomings as we are accepting of the history and meaning of our Blackness.

Unlike our academically-acculturated colleagues of color, we conscious Black poets know and advocate the necessity of poets personally participating in organized struggle and of consciously putting our politics in our art. For us, for our poetry, for our people, we are voluntarily engaged in a revolutionary struggle not just to lyrically reflect our reality, but more importantly we strive to hotly critique ourselves and our conditions in order to emotionally inspire our audiences to challenge and change reality.

The most honest of us recognize that the African-American self is deeply conflicted (perhaps "afflicted" would be a more accurate description) and thus, not all of our stories are pretty pictures. There is a stream of bitterness and bile which pollutes the rivers we have known. Being Black is difficult—beautiful, exhilarating and vital, surely—but also very, very difficult. And our poetry does not flinch from confronting the depth and breadth of our social and personal difficulties.

A journey into Blackness is both complex and complicated. We are in a state of constant becoming—an evolution that requires us to amputate cancerous appendages which aliens have grafted onto us, while we simultaneously reattach redemptive-psychic bones and rejuvenating-cultural flesh. We must both deconstruct and reconstruct our Blackness, both cut and suture.

While most of us can understand that we must each internally destroy our addiction to the security-drug of remaining a modern day consumer slave and/or welfare-ward of the state, there is an infinitely rougher mountain to ascend: the struggle to destroy the fool's goal of our desire to become a master; the longing to live in the master's house, sleep in the master's bed, dream the master's dreams and fulfill the master's fantasies.

Both we and our poetry are clear. We must either destroy our wretchedness or be destroyed by it. Deconstructing our wretchedness and reconstructing our human potential is a midnight and a crossroads that only we can experience. Whether personally as an individual or publicly as a people, there can be no proxies in the confrontation with one's soul. Each person/people must deal with the internal destruction of her/his or their own oppressed/socially-determined sense of self and also deal with the resurrection of the individually and collectively dormant, self-determining Black self.

As a result of our struggles with the selves slavery forced us to become and our struggles to become the productive people the status quo seeks to prevent, there is an irrepressible and undeniable political edge to the sentiments expressed in 360°. Passions about social situations are flying all up through here. But there is also a vim, vigor, verve and insouciant élan manifested in the smiling Black improvisational approach to dealing with the complexities and contradictions of life on planet Earth. Yes, we seriously mean to be free, but we also seriously mean to have some fun in life.

Sometimes tunnel-visioned, mainstream-oriented teacher/coaches be stressing so-called "fundamentals" so much there be no flash and dash, no improvisation and risk taking. Everything be by the numbers and no between-the-legs moves. Yeah, yeah, we know the complaint, "You guys would rather look good than win." Well, extra, extra, get the news: looking good is winning because the true essence of the game is in how well you play and not in corporate competition. Moreover, even if the bottom line were the main point, we would cop that too, if we would get to put together teams of our own choosing. We would be terrible, treacherous and nothing to mess with. Which is, finally, what 360° is.

***

360° is a challenge to those who deprecate struggle as an intimate and inseparable part of art.

Most contemporary poets are trained to disdain politics, advocacy, ideology and socially committed poetry. Some presuppose that any poet who advocates a specific politics is either more politician than poet — an unwitting, self-deluding dupe — or is voluntarily restricting their vision and craft. We know how slippery the slope is when one tries to surmount the mountain of poetic artistry while toting a backpack of social concerns. However, the difficulty of the ascension is no reason to eschew the challenge of climbing.

That old warning not to mix politics and poetry is itself an unpoetic backward line. How can anyone be a true poet, a true lover of beauty and goodness, and not be actively opposed to exploitation and oppression?

Suffice it to say, there has never been any literature that did not contain and advocate (although not necessarily consciously so) a very specific ideology either upholding or opposing the regimes of its time. Art either kisses ass or kicks ass—either way, all art is political, and it's been that way since the beginning. In that regard, 360° is a continuation of an age-old tradition that stretches back to Egypt/Africa where writing was invented. Given our alpha-esque antecedents, there should be no surprise that 360° is a dazzling quilt of conscious and cultured Black poetics. After all, Africans invented poetry, some thousands of years ago. The poets in here are just nobly and boldly upholding our ancient tradition.

***

We love language, love using language, love a mouthful of words artfully said, love poetry. The love of art is a major part of what 360° is about. For us revolution and love are inseparable, politics and art are two sides of the same coin.

A 360° appreciation of poetry includes an advocacy of sounding. Sounding is both an aesthetic and a confrontation. As an aesthetic, we inject the passion of nommo, the power of the spoken word, into our work. Even though these verses are in a book, this book is only a lead sheet, a memory device to facilitate dissemination and to assist others in articulating these neo-griot verses.

Our poems are not complete until uttered and heard, called out and responded to. Our poetry can not be fully understood in contemplative silence. Indeed, if you are somewhere alone reading this book, if you intone with your voice, your ears will hear aspects your eyes alone can never perceive.

Sounding is an aesthetic which has also been part of poetry since the beginning. Even Euro-centric poetry was initially sounded/sung, and only in industrial times has sound been muted entirely to text. The industrial tearing out of poetry's oral tongue has been so thorough in scholastic quarters that some modern poetry is impossible to declaim, impossible to follow, impossible to read aloud and sound human rather than sound bookish. Although a book doesn't really sound, to sound bookish means to ignore mouth music (the mechanics of words rolling off the palate, the confluence and clashes of vowels and consonants) in favor of intellectual stimulation sans the five senses , or six, if you count spiritual awareness as a sense.

Much of modern American poetry is as inviting as tongue licking the hot-steel, pigeon-shit-encrusted exteriors of urban skyscrapers. 360° has a different sound. 360° is in tune with the lyricism the human voice is capable of achieving when rhythm-and-melody oriented. Such lyricism is especially evident when the melody is blues-inflected. Hence, in our poetry we achieve rhythm *and* blues, which is itself a cogent description of black spirituality.

Like most of Black life, Black poetry emphasizes the harmony of movement tempered by the wisdom of irony. We poetically articulate movement by the innovative use of rhythm and rhyme. Our poetry dances. We also favor talking about something, whether making sense or nonsense, we be dropping phrases that are eminently repeatable as slogans for hip observations on the absurdities, desecrations, contradictions and occasional joys of everyday life, or as our young folk might say today, Black poetics is phunky, phat and all that!

Black poetry is popular poetry, meaning precisely that whether college-educated or street-wise, people like to hear Black poetry. Our audiences react to poetry readings as if they were in church, in a nightclub, or in bed with a lover. We bring a negroidal noise to the notion of literature. Our "literature" is a fresh and wholistic marriage of ear and eye, voice and text, aesthetics and politics. Thus, in both political emphasis and aural emphasis, our sounding is revolutionary.

***

360° is a revolution in Black poetry because we are grappling with the concrete articulation of a self-defined aesthetic grounded in the history and expressions of our people. Without a doubt, our sense of good and beauty must be distilled from our people, from our history, our present, our dreams, from us. From us must come whatever will finally be truly good and authentically beautiful for us—and that is so for all peoples, beauty and truth are always self-referential and self-defined.

African-American cultural aesthetics and practices have been the dominant force in 20th-century life worldwide. Everywhere, the air is Black with our music. People move inspired by our dance, the way we style and profile. Black art is world art!

The Black aesthetic is no mere morbid and myopic preoccupation with racial concerns. Instead, Black poetics is a 360° take on the world, a take grounded in an appreciation of Blackness, but also and equally important, our Black aesthetic is influential on and relevant to all of humanity.

While we recognize that we are neither less nor more profound than anyone else, we do unequivocally assert that we, as a people, are profound and universally influential. And here we are not engaging in sophistry or some specious self-congratulatory delusions. We know and acknowledge that we are both fierce and fucked-up, both wonderful and wack. Nevertheless, we must always remember that the depths of our contemporary problems do not negate the power and reach of our cultural influence. We are the most powerful "powerless" people in history!

Our problems may be deep, but just as we are deep enough to survive, we are also deep enough to elevate ourselves and the world with the transcendence of our art and struggle. Self-conscious art and struggle is what 360° is about!

The poets of 360° are clear about where we stand and what we are doing. Thank you for checking us out. Please join us as we turn the wheel of life 360° and then some more. This is only a(nother) beginning—a continuation of an ancient and influential tradition, actually. There is more, much, much more to come—to be continued, surely.

—Kalamu ya Salaam